The OFF-THE-BEATEN-PATH Job Book

The OFF-THE-BEATEN-PATH Job Book

You CAN Make a Living AND Have a Life!

Sandra Gurvis

A Citadel Press Book
Published by Carol Publishing Group

A Citadel Press Book
Published by Carol Publishing Group
Citadel Press is a registered trademark of Carol Communications, Inc.
Editorial Offices: 600 Madison Avenue, New York, N.Y. 10022
Sales and Distribution Offices: 120 Enterprise Avenue, Secaucus, N.J. 07094
In Canada: Canadian Manda Group, One Atlantic Avenue, Suite 105, Toronto, Ontario M6K 3E7
Queries regarding rights and permissions should be addressed to Carol Publishing Group, 600 Madison Avenue, New York, N.Y. 10022

Carol Publishing Group books are available at special discounts for bulk purchases, sales promotion, fund-raising, or educational purposes. Special editions can be created to specifications. For details, contact: Special Sales Department, Carol Publishing Group, 120 Enterprise Avenue, Secaucus, N.J. 07094

Manufactured in the United States of America

10 9 8 7 6 5 4 3 2 1

Library of Congress Cataloging-in-Publication Data

Gurvis, Sandra.
The off-the-beaten path job book / by Sandra Gurvis
p. cm.
"A Citadel Press book."
ISBN 0-8065-1644-5 (pbk.)
1. Vocational guidance. 2. Self-employed. 3. Small business.
I. Title.
HF5381.G919 1995
331.7'02—dc20 94-45276
CIP

To Ron, with thanks for your support, love, and assistance with the phone bill.

To Amy and Alex, may you always follow your chosen paths.

Contents

Acknowledgments

A book such as this would not be possible without the dozens of people affiliated with the various jobs and associations who provided leads and insights; the librarians and others at the Columbus Metropolitan Library who helped fill in the cracks with essential details; and publications such as the U.S. Government's *Occupational Outlook Handbook* and the VGM career series published by the National Textbook Company. Other useful books included the *Encyclopedia of Associations* (Gale Research) and the *Standard Periodical Directory* (Oxbridge Communications). In particular, I'd like to thank Janet Attard, Sandra Cronin-Radebaugh, Sally Fekety, Dave Flory, Nancy Grant, Mike Harden, and Mac MacLachlan. Their suggestions led to some great information.

My agent, Bert Holtje, and editors Eileen Cotton (initially) and Jim Ellison (through the bulk of the project) were, as always, immensely helpful. And although my cats Teddy and Cleo attempted to interfere with the writing process by sitting on my lap or on top of my notes, they provided welcome comic relief.

> The best careers advice . . . "Find out what you like doing best and get someone to pay you for doing it."
>
> —KATHARINE WHITEHORN

Introduction

Job Realities for the Nineties and Beyond

The Organization Man—the WASP who devoted thirty years to a single company—is washed up. He's being replaced with a tide of culturally diverse, talented people who no longer regard his as the ideal career path. According to experts, by the year 2000, 80–90 percent of workers will be women, blacks, and other so-called minorities.

The widespread availability of computer technology, an aging work force, and the increased demand for health care and other service occupations have all led to the decline of occupations such as clerks, stenographers, and machine operators. The traditional office, with its pecking order of bosses, underlings, and rigid mores may be going the way of the dinosaur.

By the late 1980s, fluctuations in the economy along with increased health care, retirement, and operating costs often made "jobs for life" impractical. Companies could not afford the expense and began laying off workers, a trend that continues today at all levels in most organizations.

The result: Employees have become free agents who flit from one "temporary" job to another or serve as consultants. Rather than conforming to strict requirements of office policy, these individuals are searching for vocations adaptable to a variety of settings, many of which are nontraditional. During their lifetimes, they may commit to one or more careers, setting aside personal funds for health care benefits and retirement plans.

An American beginning a career in the nineties will likely work in more than ten jobs with at least five employers. He or she may steer clear of the long work weeks and demanding "fast track" careers that eat up time and energy. Flexible hours and being able to work at home may be more desirable than a huge paycheck.

For many, a child's baseball game or a favorite hobby has become equally or possibly more important than hours spent toiling in an office for a remote, faceless corporation. Even better, some turn their avocations into profitable careers. The media is full of success stories about, say, the cookie maker who baked her way onto the American stock exchange.

The Off-The-Beaten-Path Job Book is intended to provide a road map to many of these possibilities. Its primary focus is on unusual and enjoyable work and where to find it. The book is organized by areas of interest—animal lovers, artistic types, computer wizards, fit and healthy, and so on. Specific occupations are then listed alphabetically underneath.

Each of the eighty-five job listings in this book consists of a brief description; the start-up costs and expected pay, necessary equipment and other requirements; and an individual case study. The job itself, money influx and output, and where to go for training and assistance are covered, as are lists of related business/trade contacts, books, and magazines.

Resources include written materials as well as advice from experts. The stories of those who have succeeded in unusual endeavors should not only provide encouragement but may spark insights and ideas. However, the chapters are meant to give an overview of the field and references are not all-encompassing. They provide a starting point rather than an encyclopedic guide.

The book directs readers to cutting-edge and burgeoning opportunities. These include traveling (as opposed to visiting) nurse, alarm systems expert, desktop publisher, image consultant, videographer, and many more. You can also learn about harder-to-find positions such as ornithologist, product tester, funeral director, and cowboy. Some categories are more specific, like holographer and polygrapher, while others, such as cruise ship worker and diet consultant, fall within a wide range of employment possibilities.

As a reader, you may locate the job of your dreams by discovering options you didn't know existed. For instance, midwifery has become a highly respected, lucrative profession, and people with even a modicum of artistic ability can earn good money as handicrafts makers. You'll get an idea of what else is out there and possibly further clarify or widen your career goals.

The Off-The-Beaten-Path Job Book is written with an eye to entertaining as well as informing readers in a variety of situations—at-home mothers exploring ways to earn a few extra dollars; executives searching for a less-pressured workplace; high school, technical school, and college graduates trying to find their niche in an already-saturated job market—just about anyone who's looking for other than the nine-to-five routine. Along with matching interests with occupations, this book steers readers to various sources for further exploration.

No one has to be unemployed or unhappy with their work—there is more than one route to professional bliss. And only in America can an individual make a living from his invention of a better pooper-scooper, while another travels the country with his troupe of cats giving seminars on training finicky felines. Work *can* be fun.

The OFF-THE-BEATEN-PATH Job Book

> Nothing is to be done really about animals. Anything you do looks foolish. It's almost as if we're put here on earth to show how silly they aren't.
>
> —RUSSELL HOBAN

Animal Lovers

Animal Care Attendant
Breeder
Dog and Cat House Builder
Groomer
Sitter/Walker
Therapist
Trainer
Veterinary Technician
Wildlife Rehabilitator

Animal Care Attendant

It's a dirty job, so you have to love it. Animal care attendants clean up blood and excrement, deal with rude and abusive owners and frantic critters, and usher animals through their final moments on Earth. Still, the work is steady and varied and the rewards are immense, especially when a deserving dog, cat, or goat is matched up with the right home. You can play with animals, nurture them, and note behavior that might indicate whether they're sick or healthy. And they don't care how you dress or behave.

Because there is such a high turnover, animal care attendants can basically pick their own venue: public or private animal shelters, veterinary hospitals or clinics, stables, laboratories, zoological parks, pet stores, aquariums, wildlife management facilities, or kennels. Attendants screen applicants for adoptions or purchase of animals; assist in routine medical procedures; and bathe, feed, and exercise their charges. They also perform clerical duties such as setting up appointments, keeping and maintaining records, and answering phones. Although shifts often involve weekends and evenings—animals don't just go away at five o'clock—many attendants work part-time.

The job doesn't pay much—around $10,000 a year to begin with, maxing out at about $30,000 for supervisory personnel. Attendants truly start at the bottom, hosing down cages and dog runs, mucking out horse stalls, and polishing saddles. Experienced attendants may do basic first aid, give shots, and perform euthanasia. Attendants need to control allergies with medication or make sure they never come in contact with the offending species. Of course, this holds true for anyone who works with animals.

Most of the training is performed on the job, so little formal education is required. Many people volunteer in clinics, zoos, or shelters and work their way up to staff positions. Still, basic courses in biology, chemistry, and physiology are helpful.

Along with requiring patience and enough sensitivity to feel compassion for animals but not freak out when they have to be put to sleep because of age, illness, or shelter policy, animal care attendants must be physically strong. You may be called upon to lift heavy boxes and bales of hay or work outside in all kinds of weather. But the outlook for this job is sunny: More and more people own dogs and cats and are demanding better care for them. Those having a strong back and warm heart might do well to start here.

Associations: Animal Caretakers Information

The Humane Society of the United States
Companion Animals Division, Suite 100
5430 Grosvenor Lane
Bethesda, MD 20814
201/452-1100 (general information)

American Boarding Kennel Association
4575 Galley Road, Suite 400-A
Colorado Springs, CO 80915
719/591-1113

American Association for Laboratory Animal Science (AALAS)
70 Timber Creek Drive, Suite 5
Cordova, TN 38018
901/754-8620

Books

Animal Caretaker. Syosset, NY: National Learning Corp., 1992.
Animal Health Aide. ibid, 1990.
Careers: Working With Animals. Hodge, Guy R. Washington, D.C.: Acropolis/HSUS, 1979.
Opportunities in Animal and Pet Care Careers. Lee, Mary Price. Lincolnwood, IL: NTC, 1994.
Veterinary Medicine and Animal Care Careers. McHugh, Mary. New York: Franklin Watts, 1977.

Magazines

Advocate
ASPCA Report
HSUS News
InterActions
Pet Gazette
Pet Health News
Shelter Sense
Shoptalk

Penny Cistaro
Animal Attendant Supervisor

In over twenty years of working at the Peninsula Humane Society and other places, Penny Cistaro of San Mateo, California, has administered a lot of euthanasia. When asked whether it bothers her, she replies, "I've seen animals tortured, hit by a car, or left outside to starve. Death is a blessing compared to suffering and abuse."

Still, she feels owners are more responsible than they used to be. "The number of stray puppies in urban areas has gone down and people are more educated about spaying and neutering." Yet as one problem disappears, others surface, such as the proliferation of feral cats. "These are the offspring of stray cats and have never known human contact. They are completely wild and dangerous and often have to be put to sleep."

Cistaro feels an animal care attendant, "must enjoy working with people and have a passion for animals. It's rewarding because you're making a difference and helping a cause." Yet even she didn't know what to tell the caller who asked her how to stop the sea gulls from flying over and defecating on his boat.

Breeder

Puppies and kittens are the primary products of professional breeders, and although baby birds, hamsters, snakes, and others have their place in the pet firmament, the first two are what most consumers prefer.

Any reputable breeder will tell you this is one way *not* to get rich. In fact, it's usually considered an expensive hobby. Costs can easily run into the thousands for kennels, everyday and travel cages, dishes, food, and starter animal(s). And this doesn't include veterinary bills, stud fees, and advertising the offspring.

In fact, possibly lucrative mass breeding (aka puppy and kitten mills) is frowned upon by organizations such as the American Kennel Club and the Cat Fancier's Association, and may prompt unannounced visits from local law enforcement agencies. Mills often produce large quantities of poor-quality animals under undesirable conditions.

A question usually asked of breeders is, "With so many stray dogs and cats, why do you continue to produce more animals?" Answers vary from wanting to improve a particular "type" (physical and genetic structure) to a professed love for a species. As a potential breeder, you need to examine your motives.

Those who decide to go ahead should talk to other breeders and join the local dog or cat club. Such support groups can provide advice and warn against pitfalls. Always make sure you purchase from, and work with, reputable breeders. There should be a need for your particular breed; a dozen ads for, say, Himalayan kittens in the newspaper of a medium-sized city is not a good sign.

You also need to be conscious of what constitutes a good "type" for your breed. Bloodlines are important as are the breeding animal's strengths and weaknesses. Beginners might do well to pick out older puppies or young adults whose characteristics have become more prominent.

The question of whether to provide stud service or get a female also needs to be addressed. Stud owners have the advantage of not having to mess with the birth as well as having the owners of the female pay travel and other expenses. The fee paid is usually the price of one puppy or kitten. However, stud owners must make sure the mating proceeds as planned (that is, monitor the actual act and intervene if necessary) and take care of the female during her stay. And it's nothing like being the social director on the *Love Boat*.

Before and during birth the animal's natural instincts take over, so owners of females often run into complications. The mother may require veterinary help or may suddenly kill or eat her offspring. And it's a rare litter in which all puppies or kittens survive.

Breeders should make sure they sell to responsible owners. Usually they keep the registration papers until they've obtained proof the dog or cat has been spayed or neutered. In the rare event a champion is produced, both breeders and their animal receive lots of recognition as well as high fees for the animal's services. And there's always the dog or cat show where the breeder can proudly display the results of his or her efforts.

Associations

American Dog Breeders Association
c/o Kate Greenwood
P.O. Box 1771
Salt Lake City, UT 84110
801/298-7513

American Kennel Club
51 Madison Ave
New York, NY 10010
212/696-8245 or
5580 Centerview Drive
Raleigh, NC 27606
919/233-9767

Cat Fanciers Association
1805 Atlantic Ave.
P.O. Box 1005
Manasquan, NJ 08736
908/528-9797

National Congress of Animal Trainers and Breeders
23675 W. Chardon Road
Grayslake, IL 60030
708/546-0717

Books

Cats. Sayer, Angela. New York: Arco, 1983.
A Feline Affair. Gilbertson, Elaine W. Loveland, CO: Alpine, 1993.
Genetics for Cat Breeders. Robinson, Roy. New York: Pergamon Press, 1977.
Practical Genetics for Dog Breeders. Willis, Malcolm B. New York: Howell, 1992.
The Standard Book of Dog Breeding. Grossman, Alvin. Fairfax, VA: Denlinger's, 1992.
Successful Dog Breeding (rev. ed). Walkowicz, Chris and Bonnie Wilcox. New York: Arco, 1985.
Veterinary Notes for Dog Breeders. Carricato, Annette M. New York: Howell House, 1992.

Magazines

American Kennel Gazette
Bloodlines
Cat World International
Dog World
K-9 Courier
Match Show Bulletin
Perspectives on Cats
Purebred Dogs

Janet Fredericks
Terrier Breeder

When Janet Fredericks of Huntington, New York, received a Jack Russell terrier as a gift for herself and her veterinarian husband, she knew she wanted to breed the species. "To me, these dogs had perfect attributes. Along with being adorable, they had delightful personalities."

But Fredericks went into it with care and a great deal of thought. "I knew what the constraints were and also had the advantage of having free medical care at home. And among breeders, you'll find splinter groups who emphasize certain physical characteristics over temperament. I'm extremely careful about the females who breed with my males. And if a puppy doesn't have the right features, I make sure it's altered."

Along with being placed with breeders and private owners all over the world, Fredericks's terriers have appeared on TV shows and in magazines. She is also the proprietor of Barnyard Babies, a traveling petting farm that includes young goats, sheep, pigs, ducklings, and other animals. "Even with all this," Fredericks says, "I just about break even. And it's nonstop constant care. But I hope I've contributed something toward healthier dogs and happier owners."

Dog and Cat House Builder

This career path can range from the simple to the sublime. At one end, you can go to a lumberyard, building supply store, or even a junkyard and get materials and pamphlets with plans and designs for rudimentary pet houses. You can basically teach yourself by reading books on carpentry, spending time with woodworkers, and building several houses on "spec." With saws, paint, sanders, and other tools, the initial investment might only be a few hundred dollars.

The houses would also benefit from extra touches such as shingles, trim, carpeting, and paint as well as tree limbs that can be used as cat scratching posts and insulation to provide protection from cold weather. With prices from $25 to $200 per house, you can generate a steady income with a clientele consisting of kennel, lumberyard, and pet store owners, who will spread the news of your wares to their customers. You might even snag a few upscale customers by constructing houses that match or complement their homes.

On the other hand, you could emulate Steven Steinheimer. A Washington, DC, architect who specializes in building scale models for architectural developers, Steinheimer is also the proprietor of Creature Comforts, which produces, four-star pet residences. Ranging in price from $4,000 for a Midwestern Barnhaus to $13,500 for San Francisco twin row houses, these canine or feline castles feature plexiglass sliding doors and windows, decks with removable plastic "pools" for food and water dishes, hardwood floors, skylights, ornamental wood finish, and even Persian rugs (for that Persian cat).

With standard brand house paints, concealed wiring, ventilation, heat, and interior lighting controlled by an exterior switch, these dwellings are built to withstand the elements. The pets' homes are constructed as well as the owners'; which is probably the reason some are the price of a small car.

Along with receiving national recognition, Steinheimer has a small but growing clientele. But a degree in architecture or extensive experience in engineering, carpentry, and design is a must for his kind of work. And unlike regular pet houses, which can be produced quickly, these customized projects require attention to minute detail and can take up to several weeks to construct.

Books

How to Build Pet Housing. Brann, Donald R. Briarcliff, NY: Directions Simplified, 1975.

Making Pet Houses, Carriers and Other Projects. Self, Charles R. New York: Sterling, 1991.

Pads For Pets. Whitney, Alex. New York: D. McKay, 1977

The Pet House Book. LaBarge, Lura. New York: Butterick, 1977.

Successful Pet Homes. Mueller, Larry. Farmington, MI: Structures, 1977.

Also handbooks and pamphlets at lumberyards and hardware stores

Magazines

American Woodworker
Crafts Magazine
Good Dog!
Weekend Woodworking Projects
Wood Projects Annual
Woodworker
Workbench Magazine

Cary Frazier
Doghouse Builder

It started out as a joke, but Cary Frazier of Bainbridge, Ohio, took to heart a suggestion in a crafts magazine that old television consoles be recycled as doghouses. "I saw a bunch of dead TV sets sitting on a curb and thought, Why not?" she recalls. "I do a lot of crafts and recycling and this seemed like a natural extension."

After leaving the set unplugged for a week ("that way, you're sure all the juice is gone"), a rubber-gloved Frazier takes out the innards, then cuts a hole in the side for a door. She replaces the screen with Plexiglas and covers the back in plywood or, for air-conditioned models, pegboard. Along with putting shingles on the roof and a heavy rubber flap over the door, Frazier strips and repaints the exterior, often making it the same color as the owner's home.

The hardest part of the houses, which range from $50 to $125, is finding an appropriate dead TV. "They have to fit and be comfortable for the dog, " she says, and are best for medium-sized pooches. But the pets really appreciate her finished product. "It gives them a view of what's going on and they don't bark as much." Frazier recently located a double console (condogminiums) and is also eyeing old stereos for possible conversion. "Anything is fair game."

Groomer

Those who really want to go to the dogs might do well to consider grooming. The job involves bathing, dematting, and drying the animal; cleaning the ears, between the pads of the feet, stomach, rectum, and eye areas; trimming whiskers and wiping out facial wrinkles; providing hot oil treatments; clipping and possibly painting nails; and, finally, cutting, scissoring, and grooming the animal's fur according to the groom pattern of the breed and preference of the owner. With nearly 150 breeds, that's a lot of learning.

Groomers may put in bows or brush and curl the fur so the Afghan or Shih Tzu more closely resembles Cousin It than the family pet. Grooming trends are geographical as well: Dogs who walk with their owners in fashionable, high-traffic areas, such as New York City, sport elaborate 'dos, while those who run outside in rural or suburban towns require practical cuts with little care.

In addition to being a dog lover, you must be a people person, and patient. In a strange and noisy environment, canines tend to be jittery. Some are biters and must be muzzled. Most respond to a gentle but firm approach and handling.

Owners are more complicated. They may be dissatisfied with the cut or want to be present during the grooming, which might distract the animal, making your job more difficult. Others may initially object to the restraints and methods necessary for grooming, falsely perceiving them as inhumane.

Although some groomers learn through apprenticeships or are self-taught, the most effective career path is to attend a trade school or classes. That way, you will be ready to either start your own business or be hired as a full-fledged groomer in an existing shop. The American Kennel Club and the local Yellow Pages list grooming schools; make sure they are licensed and accredited before signing up. Training should also provide plenty of hands-on experience, with programs taking from several weeks to almost a year for a Saturday course. Costs usually run into the low four figures.

Other expenses include something in the area of three hundred dollars for combs, barber-quality scissors, electric clippers with blades, and other grooming supplies. Those opening their own shops have the added cost of special tables, cages, sinks, and additional equipment. But grooming also pays well—about $20 an hour in the Midwest and South for experienced professionals, much more ($50,000 a year and up) for those who run successful shops. Lucrative sidelines also include selling pet care products, offering "groom-mobiles" that service pets at the owner's home, and even boarding pets. Groomers may also work in pet stores, for veterinarians, and from their homes.

Since you're on the front lines with the public, knowledge of the latest trends and cuts is necessary. Many groomers participate in ongoing training programs and keep abreast by reading trade journals. The warm months and holidays are the busiest—you may even find yourself shaving a cat or two during the "dog days" of summer.

Associations

The National Dog Groomers Association of America
Box 101
Clark, PA 11613
412/962-2711

Books

The All Breed Dog Grooming Guide. Kohl, Sam. New York: Prentice-Hall, 1987.

Grooming Dogs For Profit. Gold, Charlotte. New York: Howell, 1986.

The Standard Book of Dog Grooming. Fenger, Diane and Arlene F. Steinle. Fairfax, VA: Denlinger, 1983.

The Stone Guide To Dog Grooming For All Breeds. Stone, Ben and Pearl. New York: Howell, 1981.

Magazines

Groom & Board
Pet Washing and Grooming

Joan Drury
Veteran Groomer

Joan Drury of Crestwood, Kentucky really enjoys her job—she's been doing it since age sixteen. "More years than I want to count," she says. "I learned from a lady who mostly worked with poodles. Things have changed; nearly every breed comes in today."

Occasionally Drury will encounter a customer who doesn't understand how his Llasa Apso got so matted. "Sometimes people don't realize the care a particular breed requires. They need to look into maintenance before purchasing an animal."

And yes, some breeds are more manageable than others. "Springer and cocker spaniels are the most difficult to handle." But even the calmer dogs have their moments, like the Irish Setter who panicked at the sound of a vacuum cleaner and went to the bathroom everywhere. "I just put a pair of my husband's boxer shorts on him and hosed him down."

Sitter/Walker

At first glance, going into someone's home and walking, feeding, and playing with Fifi or Puffball seems like the ultimate easy job. But not only must pet sitters be bonded and have commercial liability insurance, they may find themselves dealing with sick and temperamental animals, armloads of paperwork, and houses where air conditioners and furnaces give out and hot water heaters break. They must also visit and exercise their charges in all kinds of weather. Although this job requires little formal education, you'll need a good dose of sense—common, business, and humor.

An estimated 60 percent of U.S. households own a dog or cat (as well as hamsters, gerbils, rabbits, frogs, and other creatures). And pet sitting has an advantage over kennel care in that animals remain in their own environment and are not exposed to diseases, thus providing the vacationing owners with greater peace of mind. Pet sitters also water plants, bring in the mail and newspaper, and turn lights off and on to deter burglars.

Depending on what the job involves and the geographical area, most sitters charge between $10 and $30 a day. Considering that the only major expenditures for established sitters are mileage and time, the profit and market potential are good. The customer provides food and supplies for the animal and is responsible for all veterinary care during the assignment.

Although the monetary investment is minimal—an answering machine, stationery and office supplies, liability insurance, and bonding costs—the cornerstone of the pet sitting business is the service contract. For a one-time fee, a lawyer can draw up a legally binding "boilerplate" contract. This will specify exactly which services the owner wants performed (for example, how many times a day the dog should be walked) as well as the pet's dietary and medical requirements and other details. Special requests, such as picking up groceries or laundry, should be charged over and above your basic fee.

Before even presenting the contract, however, visit the client's home. That way, you get to meet the pet and familiarize yourself with its environment and habits. Each pet is different, and some, such as elderly or young animals, will need more care. Other pets may be too temperamental or rowdy to handle.

Part of the beauty of pet sitting is that you can work as much as you like, from your own home or for a business employing several other sitters. But count on being busiest during the summer months and at meal times, although some customers with demanding schedules want a sitter on a year-round basis. And although the real consumers of your services can't talk back, you should also have a basic knowledge of veterinary medicine so you can truly say they're doing fine.

Associations

National Association of Pet Sitters
1200 G Street, NW
Washington, DC 20005
202/393-3317

Pet Sitters International
418 E. King Street
King, NC 27071
910/983-9222

Books

The Cat Care Manual. Viner, Bradley. Hauppauge, NY Barron's Educational Series, 1986.
Dogwatching. Morris, Desmond. New York: Crown, 1987.
Pet Sitting for Profit. Moran, Patti. New York: Howell, 1991.
The Very Healthy Cat Book. Belfield, W.O. and M. Zucker. New York: McGraw-Hill, 1983

Magazines

Family Pet
Pet Age
Pet Business Magazine

Lydia Foro
Pet Sitter

Lydia Foro of Glendale, Arizona, differs from most pet sitters: She usually takes only one client at a time. "I literally come in and stay with the animal overnight," she says. Consequently, her fees range from $25 to $40 per day instead of the usual $15. "But customers know their pet is getting the same pampering as if they were there themselves."

Foro has approximately fifty clients. "In this business, references are important. Anyone can call himself a pet sitter and even get a (vendor's) license."

She recommends affiliation with associations, along with continuous expansion of knowledge. "The Humane Society of the United States offers conferences and expos. College courses and seminars on animal care are always available."

Therapist

To many, the idea of a pet therapist to analyze their dog's or cat's problems seems amusing. But pet therapists go through years of training in experimental psychology, anatomy, zoology, and veterinary science. Those certified by the Animal Behavior Society (ABS) have completed specific doctoral programs (currently given at the University of California-Davis, the University of Georgia, and Texas A & M) or related programs, and have at least five years experience in the field. They are expected to adhere to the ethical codes of the American Psychological Association and the ABS.

Along with spending much time and money on education, pet therapists need to take out liability insurance. The premiums vary, depending on whether they have their own facility or visit the pet at home. Most therapists prefer the latter; it gives them an idea of the animal's environment. Therapists wishing to set up an office need to consider the expense of that as well.

Because their direct competition is dog trainers and obedience schools, which are usually less costly, therapists often confer with veterinarians for referrals, rather than advertise in the Yellow Pages or use other standard methods. As therapists become more established, pet owners also provide recommendations.

Along with dogs and cats, animal therapists may specialize in horses, birds, farm and zoo animals, even wolves, coyotes, and bison. They study the animals' habits and environment, and publish their findings in professional journals. They can teach and do research in colleges, for the government, and at zoos, aquariums, and for conservation groups. Salaries vary widely according to the type of job.

Many, however, choose to work directly with animals in a therapeutic setting. They can charge from $300 to $500 for a six-week program for dogs (including phone consultations that continue after treatment is finished) and from $150 to $300 for cats, which are easier to handle. Therapists can bolster their incomes by providing expert testimony regarding the reasons for animal misbehavior, consulting for vets and zoos, and through community outreach services, such as classes on understanding your pet.

As a therapist, you may find yourself doing everything from teaching pigs how to regulate their body temperature (by pressing a lever that turns on heat) to prescribing valium for cats so they can relearn proper litter habits.

Associations

Animal Behavior Society
Mercer University
Department of Psychology
1400 Coleman Ave.
Macon, GA 31207
912/752-2973

International Association of Human-Animal Interactions
Century Building, Suite 303
321 Burnett Ave. S.
Renton, WA 98057
206/226-7357

Books

Becoming Best Friends. Leon, Jane. New York: Berkley, 1993.
Between Pets and People. Beck, Alan M. New York: Putnam, 1983.
Cats on the Couch. Wilbourn, Carole. New York: Collier-Macmillan, 1992.
Is Your Cat Crazy? Wright, John and Judi Wright Lashnits. New York: Macmillan, 1994.

Magazines

Animal Behavior Consultant Newsletter
Animal Behaviour
Behaviour
Behavioral Ecology
The Journal of Comparative Psychology

John Wright
Animal Behavior Specialist

Dr. John Wright of Mercer University in Macon, Georgia began his career studying aggression in mice. But today, along with writing a book on cat behavior and helping found the ABS, he has a thriving pet therapy practice. And he makes house calls.

Once Wright and the owner agree on a course of treatment, he goes to the person's home and provides a complete workup—diagnosis, behavioral history, and therapy program, in which he shows family members how to react around the pet and how his approach is going to operate. He does follow-up visits and phones weekly until the behavior problem is resolved.

"I'm usually the last resort," he says. "The owner has exhausted all avenues—he's had the animal checked with the veterinarian to make sure the problem isn't physical, and obedience training has failed. By now, both he and his pet are pretty anxious."

Wright's job often involves detective work. "Something in the house may be upsetting the animal or it picks up an aberrant behavior pattern. It's a matter of reconditioning and retraining."

Trainer

Although animal trainers can make from $25,000 to $50,000 a year, *they* must have proper training. And because no strict professional or educational standards have been established, obtaining the right credentials can be tricky.

There are several routes: college courses in psychology, animal behavior/science, and veterinary technology; programs established by the armed services; dog training academies; and apprenticeship at an existing facility. However, academy courses are usually short, running three to twelve months, with students cleaning kennels and receiving only very basic instruction. And volunteer apprenticeships should be selected with care, as some facilities are more creditable than others. Along with their reputation, you'll need to examine their methods and philosophy as well as how they deal with disobedient animals.

After you get your training, you can work with assist dogs to help the blind and those otherwise incapacitated; with drug enforcement and rescue canines for military, police, or other government agencies; or with purebreds needing professional handlers for various shows. Sometimes it comes down to a preference for rottweilers over poodles.

Often trainers offer obedience classes in addition to working with individual pets. They can then add to their income by boarding animals and distributing pet care products. Others work with guard dogs for private purchasers. These animals can "fetch" burglars, along with an asking price of up to $5000.

And don't forget the performing arts, whose trained-animal needs are extending beyond felines and canines. Producers, zookeepers, aquarium curators, and circus and other show organizers may all need your services. Finding the next Mr. Ed or Bonzo could mean big bucks. Those who wish to train horses have the prestige of participating in various competitions and races.

As an animal trainer, you can be an independent contractor or work for someone else. You also set your own hours. But just remember that although you're communing with your best friends, it's their owners who sign your check.

Associations

The American Equine Association
Box 658
Newfoundland, NJ 07435
201/697-9668

Assistance Dogs International
c/o Robin Dickson
10175 Wheeler Road
Central Point, OR 97502
503/826-9220

Cat Fancier's Association
1805 Atlantic Ave.
P.O. Box 1005
Manasquan, NJ 08736
908/528-9797

International Cat Association
P.O. Box 2684
Harlingen, TX 78551
512/428-8046

The National Association of Dog Obedience Instructors
2286 E. Seel Road
St. Johns, MI 48879
517/224-8683

The Professional Handlers' Association (dogs only)
15810 Mount Demarast Lane
Silver Spring, MD 20906
301/924-0089

Books

The Complete Book of Dog Obedience. Saunders, Blanche. New York: Howell, 1978
Dog Problems. Benjamin, Carol Lea. New York: Howell, 1989.
The Educated Cat. Ney, George with Susan Fadem. New York: E.P. Dutton, 1987.
Educating Horses From Birth to Riding. Jones, Peter. New York: Howell, 1986.
The Gentle Jungle. Helfer, Toni R. Provo, Utah: Brigham Young University, 1980.
Train Your Cat. Jester, Terry. New York: Avon, 1992.

Magazines

Cat Fancy
Cat World
Dog Fancy
Dog World
Horse Show
Horse World

George Ney
Cat Trainer

George Ney of Mundelin, Illinois, logs forty thousand miles annually with his troupe of performing cats. They roll over, play dead, jump through hoops, answer the phone, and do other feats at cat expos, old age homes, children's hospitals, and TV stations. The purring players have been on stage at the Cow Palace in San Francisco and have appeared in ads for Nyquil, Chevrolet, Hallmark Cards, and many cat products.

According to Ney, training cats requires two things: love and patience. "Cats have a very short attention span and must enjoy being handled," he observes. "You also use signals—for instance, putting your hand on the cat's rear when you want him to sit down—and offer positive reinforcement, such as praise and treats."

What does Ney do when his cats are having a bad fur day and refuse to perform? "Well, I understand that the audience is on the side of the cat, particularly when the cat gives me a drop-dead look. But I'm always able to finish the show, even if it's on the cat's terms and not my own."

Veterinary Technician

A leap up from animal attendant is veterinary technician (VT, or vet tech), which, in addition to a high school degree, requires two years of academic training. Along with a core curriculum of chemistry, applied mathematics, communications skills, and biological science, courses cover ethics, anatomy/physiology, biochemistry, animal husbandry, and many other subjects. Summers are usually spent working in a clinic or an animal shelter, often without pay or at minimum wage. After receiving an Associate in Applied Science or a similar degree, and depending upon the local requirements, you may also have to take an exam to become registered or certified by your employing state.

In fact, the American Veterinary Medical Association, which accredits the approximately sixty-five VT programs in the

United States, recommends a strong high school science background. So those interested in this career can start getting ready for it during their fifth-grade science fair.

Most vet techs work in private practices. But they can also find employment in biological research facilities, drug or feed manufacturing companies, animal production facilities, zoos, and—not for vegetarians—meat packing companies. They keep records, take care of and feed the animals, do laboratory procedures and equipment maintenance, help with research projects, and inspect carcasses.

Those employed by doctors obtain and record information about pets and their owners; collect specimens and do routine laboratory procedures; prepare animals, instruments, and equipment for surgery; provide nursing care; work with X-rays; and assist in diagnosis and surgery. In other words, they do just about everything the vet doesn't.

Along with specialized skills, the most important thing a vet tech can possess is empathy—both for the animal and its owner. As with human ailments, a lot of stress is involved, requiring patience and understanding. And it often falls on the vet tech to do basic paw-holding and explaining to owners.

For all the hard work and long hours—evenings and weekends, and the inevitable emergency traffic of patients at the end of the day—compensation is just adequate. Vet techs earn more than animal attendants, with starting pay between $13,000 and $16,000 a year. There's also a shortage of formally trained technicians. So this career path looks promising, even if it is littered with sick animals.

Associations

American Association of Laboratory Animal Science
70 Timber Creek Drive, Suite 5
Cordova, TN 38018
901/754-8620

American Veterinary Medical Association
1931 N. Meacham Rd., Suite 100
Schaumburg, IL 60173
708/925-8070

Books

Animal Health Technician Licensing Examination. Syosset, NY: National Learning Corp., 1990.
Review Questions and Answers for Veterinary Technicians. Goleta, CA: American Veterinary Publications, 1993.
See also Animal Attendant

Magazines

Veterinary Practice Staff
Veterinary Technician

Lynne Stratton
Licensed Veterinary Technician

Lynne Stratton of Ypsilanti, Michigan, originally planned on being a veterinarian but changed her mind when she realized she didn't want to make life and death decisions. She became a vet tech instead, and now teaches courses on animal care at the local college in addition to working at an emergency clinic.

Stratton likes the fact that she's in constant contact with animals. "Basically, most of them are terrified when they come in. So, after a while, you learn to read their signals and can approach them in a nonthreatening manner." In her fifteen years as a vet tech, she's never been bitten on the job.

A drawback is that most technicians must provide their own insurance. "The vets get insurance through their association so VTs must either be self-insured or on their spouse's company policy." An offsetting fact is that at least their *animals* are covered: "We get medicines at cost and don't have to pay for office visits.

"People just starting out don't realize they must learn about all of the species, not just dogs and cats," she observes. "So they need to be able to deal with horses, even if they don't like them. You never know what's going to walk through that door and require treatment."

Wildlife Rehabilitator

Those who envision this job as rescuing Bambi, Thumper, et al. and taking them home to the kids should best think again. Wildlife rehabilitators are called in when species are displaced or harmed by oil spills, urban sprawl, highway construction, illegal hunting or poaching, or other unnatural disasters. Creatures are often severely traumatized and affected by the "flight or fight" syndrome. With wounds, broken bones, and damage from poison, they require special handling and care.

This job requires an ability to placate and handle wild creatures—not an easy feat. Hazards include bites, scratches, and preparation of really disgusting food, such as ground-up fish for birds. You need to know about species behavior patterns, medications, first aid, shock cycles, and proper caging and care. And along with training in biology, veterinary science, and physical therapy, you may also need a permit to work as a rehabilitator, depending upon local government regulations. Requirements can include performance evaluations, internships, written exams, and continuing education credits.

Jobs can be found at public or private rehabilitation centers in forests, parks, or agencies, even on ranches or farms. Professional rehabilitators make from $12,000 to $40,000 annually, depending upon geographical location and supervisory duties. Since animals need round-the-clock care, you may also be provided with housing on the grounds of the center.

Rehabilitators usually start as volunteers, then obtain specialized and on-the-job training. Tasks may range from cleaning and caring for creatures caught in oil spills to setting up a physical therapy program for a specific species to doing blood work and urinalysis. The work is demanding, difficult, and can result in burnout.

With the unfortunate increase of air, water, and land pollution, the demand for skilled rehabilitators is great. And you may be the last fragile link to a species' survival.

Associations

International Wildlife Rehabilitation Council
4437 Central Place, Suite B-4
Suisun, CA 94585
707/864-1761

Wildlife Information Center
629 Green Street
Allentown, PA 18102
215/433-1637

The Wildlife Society
5410 Grosvenor Lane
Bethesda, MD 20814
301/897-9770

Books

Care of the Wild. Jordan, W.J. New York: Rawson, 1983

Care of the Wild Feathered and Furred. Hickman, Mae. New York: Michael Kensend, 1993.

The Complete Care of Orphaned or Abandoned Baby Animals. Spaulding, C. E. Emmaus, PA: Rodale, 1979.

First Aid and Care of Wildlife. Martin, Richard M. North Pomfret, NJ: David and Charles, 1984.

Out of the Wild. Tomkies, Mike. London: Cape, 1992.

Rescue and Rehabilitation of Oiled Birds (microfiche). Welte, Sallie. Washington, DC: U.S. Department of Interior, Fish and Wildlife Service, 1991.

Magazines

InterActions
Mainstream
Wildlife Rehabilitation Today
NWRA Quarterly
Journal of Wildlife Rehabilitation
Wildlife Journal

Pat DeLong
Backyard Rehabilitator

Rehabilitator Pat DeLong lives on six acres of wooded terrain in Dexter, Michigan. As a member of Friends of Wildlife, an Ann Arbor-based group of about 170 volunteers, DeLong says, "we feel like we're making a difference. We can help thousands of fox, deer, coyotes, and other mammals." Like many such organizations, their efforts are funded by various community outreach projects.

DeLong's days revolve around the care of her charges. "I start at 9:00 AM, and feed them every four hours, even if I'm up the night before doing IVs." Cages must be cleaned, formula mixed, and other special needs attended to. "It never stops."

DeLong warns against the hazards of imprinting (or attachment), citing the example of a man who adopted a pet squirrel only to have his neighbor hit the animal with a shovel after it ran up the man's leg. "We put on nature audios when we feed animals and use a bottle rack whenever possible. The point is to have the animal function on its own."

> If Botticelli were alive today, he'd be working for Vogue.
>
> —PETER USTINOV

Artistic Types

Art Conservator
Calligrapher
Cartoonist/Caricaturist
Handicrafts Maker
Illustrator
Interior Designer
Jewelry Appraiser
Tattoo Artist
Window Merchandiser

Art Conservator

Today's art conservator is far more than a frustrated painter assigned to touch up a Rembrandt or a Van Gogh. This field also encompasses museum and historical exhibits, sculpture, photographs, books, textiles, and more, with the relatively unexplored fields of musical instruments and technological artifacts needing conservation skills as well. In addition to a college degree with emphasis on chemistry, the humanities, and studio art, conservators serve apprenticeships and also take specialized graduate programs of two to four years. And then—maybe—they get a job stretching canvas or working on samples.

Experienced conservators will tell you it takes five to ten years of additional toil in a professional facility to grasp the nuances of various techniques. Most conservators specialize—the requirements for restoring frescoes are quite different from those for paper items, for instance. In this job there are no second chances, so conservators are trained to handle items with the greatest care.

Beginners usually work at museums or in conservation laboratories, which are either individually owned or supported by larger institutions. Average annual pay starts at around $20,000, with mid-level jobs reaching into the $40,000 range. After a few years, you can branch out on your own and, if you're extremely good, command a salary approaching six figures. Other positions can be found in regional facilities, heritage centers, libraries, universities, archives, and in public and private enterprises.

To the untrained eye, the handiwork of conservators may not look impressive. But their goal is to return an object to its original form, rather than alter it. They examine cultural properties and assess their condition, judging the extent of damage; analyze and research the origin of the item to determine how best to stabilize it; and then record the conditions of the artifact before, during, and after treatment. They minimize deterioration by providing controlled environments.

In addition to an appreciation of a variety of cultural properties, conservators need an aptitude for the scientific and technical, since they tend to work with all types of equipment, materials, and chemicals, some of which are toxic. And fantasies of being the next Grandma Moses or Marc Chagall can be checked at the door—the work can be tedious and requires a great deal of attention to detail. Since each situation is so vastly different and usually requires a decision by a committee, conservators must also be able to make sound judgments and communicate their recommendations.

Although competition can be keen, the field is wide open. Prospects can only increase as more art objects age and require restoration, and as the public becomes increasingly aware of the need for conservation. And you'll have a chance to work with some of the most impressive achievements of humankind—as long as you don't drop anything.

Associations

American Institute for Conservation of Historic and Artistic Works
1717 K Street, NW, Suite 301
Washington, DC 20006
202/452-9545

Association for Preservation Technology
P.O. Box 8178
Fredericksburg, VA 22404
703/373-1621

International Council of Monuments and Sites, U.S. Committee
Decatur House
1600 H Street, NW
Washington, DC 20006
202/842-1866

National Institute for the Conservation of Cultural Property
3299 K Street, NW, Suite 403
Washington, DC 20007
202/625-1495

National Trust for Historic Preservation
Office of Preservation Services
1785 Massachusetts Ave., NW
Washington, DC 20036
202/673-4000

Books

The Art of the Conservator. Oddy, Andrew, ed. Washington, D.C.: Smithsonian, 1992.
Caring for Your Art. Snyder, Jill. New York: Allworth, 1990.
Caring for Your Collections. New York: Abrams, 1992.
Guide to Degree Programs in Historic Preservation. Washington, DC: National Trust for Historic Preservation, annual.
Guidelines for Selecting a Conservator. Washington, DC: American Institute for Conservation of Historic and Artistic Works, 1991.
The Nature of Conservation: A Race Against Time. Ward, Philip. Marina Del Ray, CA: Getty Conservation Institute, 1989.

Magazines

The Abbey Newsletter
IIC Studies in Conservation
JAIC Journal
The Paper Conservator
Technology and Conservation

Dianne van der Reyden
Paper Conservator

Dianne van der Reyden of the Smithsonian Institution often finds herself in the role of detective. “It’s important to understand why an object deteriorates,” she observes. “Along with a grasp of the composition of the material, you almost need forensic ability.” In addition to extensive library research, she utilizes microscopes, ultraviolet lights, even X-rays to make her determinations. “Along with the more traditional methods, we use the latest technological advances, such as enzymes and modern synthetic materials for protection.”

But there's nothing like the excitement of discovering the real thing, such as her recent attempt to verify a Michelangelo drawing. "Basically, we matched the water marks on the paper with those characteristic of the time period." They then very cautiously removed the mounting—any kind of interference could ruin it forever—and discovered another original drawing on the back.

Van der Reyden also helps the public with their own conservation projects. "People are always wanting to know how to preserve scrapbooks, albums, even newspaper clippings. There are certain steps to slow down the deterioration process. In a sense, conservation is a lot like human life support."

Calligrapher

If you can't draw a straight line or got a D in penmanship (like yours truly), turn the page. Otherwise, calligraphy can provide an excellent outlet for creative skills while staying at home. Start-up costs are minimal—pens, pen nibs, ink, a T-square, and fine quality paper (although that's often supplied by clients). Those investing in a home computer and pen plotter that provides calligraphic images might have to pay a few thousand dollars more—and what's the point in learning a craft unless you do it yourself?

This field lends itself to lots of different outlets—addressing envelopes for social events, although computers have taken a bite out of that; providing "fill-ins," for diplomas, certificates, and preprinted invitations; lettering signs; and preparing mechanicals for items that are to be printed. Calligraphers also create original documents for churches, companies, schools, and individuals. Jobs may involve everything from business logos to greeting cards to T-shirts.

Calligraphy can be found on almost every ink-bearing surface—all types and quality of paper, cardboard, fabric, even on wood, glass, and ceramics. And the writing styles are infinite, ranging from subtle hand-block lettering to ornate curlicues and tails. Although there are dozens of specific forms (gothic, roman, italic, uncial, blackletter) lettering can be as individual as the calligrapher herself, expressing a range of emotions from reverence to sorrow to joy.

Calligraphy may sound easy (even a dumb computer can address invitations, right?), but professionals recommend at least two years' study with a journeyman instructor, art classes from a local college, adult education programs, or a combination of these. You can also dip into it with the nearest guild (there are over one hundred in the United States), which will provide you with resources and guidance.

Pay is in the $25-per-hour range for those with a proven record, considerably less for beginners. Calligraphers in big cities usually charge more. Most hang out their beautifully lettered shingles as freelancers, although a few full-time positions can be found at card companies, printing enterprises, and in diplomatic and government agencies, such as the White House. Print shops, graphics arts firms, and publishers are good sources of part-time work.

It takes practice to develop the confidence, patience, and steady hand required to create consistently beautiful lettering. There's little room for error here, although bleach, water-soluble white paint, typewriter correction fluid, razor blades, and electric erasers can work wonders. Just hope the client doesn't notice.

Associations

Friends of Calligraphy
P.O. Box 5194
San Francisco, CA 94101
408/429-8849

International Association of Master Penmen and Teachers of Handwriting (IAMPTH)
19125 Southwest 107th Lane
Dunnellon, FL 34432
904/489-9468

Society for Calligraphy
P.O. Box 64174
Los Angeles, CA 90064
213/931-6146

Society of Scribes
P.O. Box 933
New York, NY 10150
(no phone)

Books

The Calligraphy Sampler. Pearce, Charles. London: Collins, 1985.

Calligraphy Techniques. Lancaster, John. London: B. T. Batsford, 1986.

Calligraphy. Davis, J. Y. and J. V. Richardson. Littleton, CO: Libraries Unlimited, 1982.

How to Become a Professional Calligrapher. David, Stuart. New York: Taplinger, 1985.

Sixty Alphabets. Briem, S., ed. New York: Thames and Hudson, 1986.

Magazines

The Calligraph
Calligraphy Review
Letter Arts Review
association newsletters

Ann Woods
Professional Calligrapher

Ann Woods of Columbus, Ohio has put her mark on all types of items, from menus to calendars, to hand-printed books. "I was always good in penmanship and loved history," she said. She first discovered calligraphy through an adult education class.

"This was something I could really delve into," she goes on. "Lettering has followed architectural styles and fashion through the ages. And not only does it require self-discipline and precision, but I have continually refined my skills over the years."

Although being an independent calligrapher requires self-discipline, Woods also enjoys the freedom. "You can put on your own interpretation in terms of spacing and letter-form structure. The possibilities are endless."

Cartoonist/Caricaturist

This is more of a calling than a job. Although formal training is readily available in art schools, through adult education classes, and in colleges, many cartoonists and caricaturists have been capturing friends, family, and political figures on paper as far back as they can remember. Motivation, persistence, and the ability to deal with rejection in the mode of the Energizer bunny have much to do with success in this field.

Although their methods of expression can be vastly different, cartoonists and caricaturists start with the same basic tool—a portfolio of their best work, which they display to potential clients, mostly newspapers and magazines. Examples should be slanted toward the desired job; you wouldn't show a risqué cartoon to *Good Housekeeping*, for example, or a politically incorrect sight gag to the *New Yorker*.

Always keep the desired audience in mind, that is, the readers of your target publications. The rendering must be easily reproducible, so study the magazine's requirements, often found in a book called *Humor and Cartoon Markets* (see below). A batch of about ten or so samples, as well as work published elsewhere, may get you a toenail hold in the door.

Once someone agrees to showcase your work, they will usually offer a set fee, which can range from $10 for one-time rights in a local market to $350 or more for a national magazine. Most cartoonists are wary of pay on publication, which can stretch to a year or two. So either get it in writing that the publication will print your rendering within a reasonable time (three months), or negotiate pay on acceptance, which means the check will be in the mail in about six weeks (maybe). Except for syndicated giants such as "Peanuts," "Cathy," "Doonesbury," and "The Far Side," few get rich in this field.

Cartoonists who desire syndication have a lot of work ahead of them before they even send out their first batch. Because syndicated cartoons usually run daily, artists must develop four to six weeks' worth of story line and characters, making sure there's continuity as well as a premise for future episodes. Art work must be camera ready. If the syndicate is interested, they may request to see enough material for another three to four weeks. And that's no guarantee of purchase. Although the day-to-day creation of a particular cartoon can be a grind, syndication can provide a steady, if not comfortable, income.

However, most cartoonists utilize their talents in other ways. Many work in caricature either for publication or as a form of entertainment. The former are often found on op-ed pages or in magazine articles about celebrities and other notables. Unlike cartoons, which stand alone, caricatures are often used to illustrate text. Artists with a flair for schmoozing and flattery may find work drawing exaggerated likenesses of those attending parties, bar mitzvahs, and corporate events. However, not everyone may like what they see, so be prepared for some negative reactions. With an average rate of $125 an hour, you can afford to take some criticism.

Associations

Cartoonist's Guild of New York
11 W. 20th Street, 8th floor
New York, NY 10011
212/348-8023

Cartoonists Northwest
P.O. Box 31122
Seattle, WA 98103
206/752-4419

National Cartoonists Society
Columbus Circle
New York, NY 10023
212/627-1550

Books

The Art of Caricature. Gautier, Dick. New York: Putnam, 1985.
The Career Cartoonist. Gautier, Dick. New York: Putnam, 1992.
Cartooning. Keener, Polly. Englewood Cliffs, NJ: Prentice-Hall, 1992.
Cartooning for Beginners. Maddocks, Peter. Secaucus, NJ: Chartwell, 1994.
The Complete Book of Caricature. Staake, Bob. Cincinnati: North Light, 1991.
Everything You Wanted To Know About Cartooning but Were Afraid To Draw. Hart, Christoper. New York: Watson-Guptill, 1994.
Humor and Cartoon Markets. Cincinnati: F & W, updated periodically.

Magazines

Cartoonist
Cartoonist Profiles
Get Stupid
Political Pix
Witty World

Joe Duffy
Freelance Cartoonist

Joe Duffy of New York City believes he was born to be a cartoonist. "My aunt worked for King Features Syndicate, so I was exposed to Milton Caniff, Rube Goldberg, and Mort Walker at an early age— and it lead to contamination," he jokes. In his many decades as a cartoonist, he has worked for newspaper syndicates, trade newsletters and journals, and general interest magazines. This Joe of all trades has also created designs for T-shirts and hats, done caricatures and greeting cards, and teaches continuing education.

Beginning artists, Duffy believes, need as much exposure as possible, even if it's sketching caricatures of passers-by at malls, county fairs, and art shows. "This builds experience," he states. "And people love to watch you draw. But never do anyone without their permission."

Success, he believes, depends on timing and flexibility. "In a way it's a lot like show business, of being in the right place. One job leads to another and the most unexpected circumstances can result in success." But mostly, he says, "You need to keep up with things, and be aware of what's going to sell. Everything is negotiable."

Handicrafts Maker

In today's styrofoam and particle-board world, there's a hunger for finely made, hand-wrought products. These can range from appliquéd designs on aprons, pot warmers, and T-shirts to wooden bookcases, picture frames, puzzles, and trivets. Beadwork, crocheting, embroidery, quilting, patchwork, and dozens of other handicrafts are also making a comeback.

You don't have to be particularly talented to be a handicrafts maker, although manual dexterity is a must, as are patience and enjoyment of the chosen medium. You can train yourself by purchasing crafts kits or how-to books (vocational and college courses and apprenticeships are available, but can be costly). Effort and raw materials are your major investment. Most craftspeople start part-time and develop a clientele.

Appropriate pricing based on actual production costs and what the market will bear is also vital. Items should be of the best quality to avoid disgruntled customers and a reputation for sloppiness. Nothing travels faster than bad news.

You then need to decide whether you want to sell your product wholesale or on consignment, go directly to the public, or, as with most craftspeople, do a combination of these. Outlets include gift and craft shops, galleries, and department stores.

Along with mail order and selling from your home/studio, arts festivals and crafts markets are other excellent sources for sales. Most major cities have several events; check with the local chamber of commerce to find out dates and places. Shows usually involve a jury system, so you'll need to apply several months in advance.

Displays at malls and farmer's markets have potential, but find out about their clientele first. The crowd at an upscale shopping mall is quite different from that at an average suburban mall and farmer's markets attract a mostly rural clientele.

If it's appealing, the item will sell itself. And you don't even have to dress up.

Associations

American Craft Council
72 Spring Street
New York, NY 10012
212/274-0030

American Crafts Alliance
425 Riverside Drive, Apartment 15-H
New York, NY
212/866-2239

Association of Crafts and Creative Industries
1100-H Brandywine Blvd.
Zanesville, OH 43702
614/452-4541

Books

Craft Making for Love or Money. Buxton, Gail. New York: Executive Communications, 1983.
Creative Cash, Brabec, Barbara. Naperville, IL: self published, 1991.
How to Sell Your Arts and Crafts. Smith, Allan H. Palm Beach Gardens, FL: Success Publications, 1989.
Start and Run a Profitable Craft Business. 4th ed. Hynes, William G. Bellingham, WA: Self-Counsel, 1992.

Magazines

American Craft
Crafts
Crafts 'N Things
Egger's Journal
Foxfire

Kathleen Johns
Eggshell Designer

Kathleen Johns of Dublin, Ohio, knows the true meaning of walking on eggs. As a creator of pysanky, traditional hand-decorated Ukrainian eggs, she turns out thousands of colorful, intricately designed works of oval art. The batik-like process involves drawing wax designs on eggs, then dyeing them. Symbolic colors and patterns are utilized, imbuing each egg with meaning. "When I first saw pysanky in my neighbor's kitchen. I fell in love with it, although at first, I wasn't very good."

But she persisted with an initial investment of about twenty dollars for beeswax, dye, and eggs, and a pysanky kit given to her by an aunt. Soon her family and friends began to praise her handiwork, spurring her to peddle some through a local store. "I was afraid no one would want them, but they were gone almost immediately."

Ranging in price from $35 to $500, Kathleen Johns's eggs sell at fine collectible and museum shops. She also travels to crafts fairs and art shows, promotes her product through speeches and interviews, and conducts workshops on pysanky. Although she now employs other artists, she still oversees the designs and colors. "Because of the process, no two eggs are exactly alike. Each is a handmade, freeform creation.

"The eggs are said to bestow good luck, health, and prosperity on the receiver," Johns continues. They seem to have done that for her—as long as she remembers to pierce tiny holes and drain them after her work is done.

Illustrator

This field comes with an enormous array of options. You can illustrate everything from an instruction manual to human anatomy and surgical procedures for medical journals, to covers for books, to the insides of magazines. Illustrations also appear on posters, stationery, greeting cards, wrapping paper, and story boards for TV commercials. Fashion illustrators depict the latest designs and scientific illustrators provide renderings of animals and plants. You can work in pencil, pastel and chalk, ink, charcoal, watercolor, gouache (opaque watercolor), airbrush, and acrylics. Even computers have their place here, as they can create many realistic or abstract versions that the illustrator can print out.

However, competition for these jobs is keen, and illustrators usually specialize. Most graduate from either an art school or receive a bachelor's degree with an emphasis on art. Medical illustrators bone up via pre-med courses and can obtain a master's degree in their field, offered by a few accredited colleges in the United States. Scientific illustrators can also take appropriate undergraduate classes, and most commercial illustrators coming out of school today are familiar with computer-aided design.

But more important than any formal training is your portfolio, which is how you get assignments. Art and design directors and others make decisions on whether to hire you based on this "best of" collection. Most beginning illustrators develop portfolios while still in school or during internships, although a few with exceptional talent may squeak by without any classes or previous experience.

Those starting out often take jobs with advertising agencies, publishing houses, design firms, or commercial art and reproduction companies. Illustrators brave enough to fly solo may find freelance employment at these and at other companies requiring their temporary services. Jobs can be obtained by word of mouth, by reading trade journals, or through the current *Artist's Market* (see below).

Pay for full-time employees is about $18,000 to $31,000 a year, with income varying widely for freelancers. The latter can contract by the hour or the job. Those with a regular set of clients can earn a healthy salary, along with getting to pick and choose their assignments. Magazine illustration fees vary, depending on whether it's a local or national publication.

Start-up costs can run into several hundred dollars, what with easels, drafting tables, drawing equipment, and supplies, as well as the expense of putting together a professional-looking portfolio. But there will always be a need for illustrators, and this is one artistic endeavor where you don't have to live in New York or Los Angeles to be a big success.

Associations

Graphic Arts Guild
11 W. 20th Street, 8th floor
New York, NY 10011
212/463-7730

National Association of Schools of Art and Design
11250 Roger Bacon Drive, Suite 21
Reston, VA 22090
703/437-0700

The Society of Illustrators
128 East 63rd Street
New York, NY 10021-7392
212/838-2560

Books

The Art of Illustration. Melot, Michael. New York: Skira/Rizzoli, 1984.

Getting Started as a Freelance Illustrator or Designer. Fleishmann, Michael. Cincinnati: North Light, 1990.

The Golden Age of Children's Book Illustration. Dalby, Richard. New York: Gallery, 1991.

The Illustrator's Handbook. Smith, Stan and H. F. Holt New York: Gallery, 1984.

Magazines

American Illustration Showcase
Applied Arts
Art Business News
Illustrator
association newsletters

Charles Santore
Children's Book Illustrator

Charles Santore of Philadelphia, began his "illustrious" career doing black-and-white drawings for a small religious publication. "Basically, I hit the streets with my portfolio, visiting several publishing concerns and advertising agencies at one time," he recalls. Once editors became familiar with his work, he began to illustrate articles for *Redbook* and other major magazines. Today he does classics (*Peter Rabbit*, *The Wizard of Oz*, *Snow White*, and others) for Random House.

Each book takes two to three years to research. "I set it in a particular time and place, so the costumes, landscape, and architecture must be authentic. Unlike a drawing that can be summed up in one image, children's books have a long narrative and build up to a crescendo, somewhat like a piece of music.

"In this business, the scale of payment has gone down over the years, so you'd better really enjoy the work."

Interior Designer

Gone is the time when, with very little formal training but with a flair for color, an interior decorator breezed into homes and work spaces, telling clients what to put in their living rooms and lobbies. Today's interior designer is a graduate of a two- or usually four-year training program emphasizing art and art history, principles of design, designing and sketching, and other specialized skills.

The latter can include space planning and cost estimating; construction drawing and specifications; contract documents and bidding procedures; furniture, fixtures, and equipment; interior construction; finishes, lighting, mechanical/electrical systems, and acoustics; building codes, exits, barrier-free design;

and owner-designer agreements, professional practice, and project coordination. Not to mention the computer-assisted design classes which teach you how to create several versions of a space, enabling customers to choose from the various options. This is not a job for a dilettante, but definitely one for a jack-of-all-trades.

Along with being creative and a good communicator (not always mutually exclusive traits) with an eye for new ideas and influences, an interior designer must also be cost-conscious. No longer the province of the wealthy and companies with unlimited budgets, designers sell themselves by giving clients more "bang for the buck." They have access to discounts and the know-how to acquire unique and hard-to-get objects. Focus is on emphasizing the client's theme and personal taste, rather than the other way around.

The field is further complicated by the necessity for strict adherence to federal, state, and local building codes; nearly twenty states (including the District of Columbia) require licensing. Designers must also be familiar with toxicity and flammability standards for furnishings. Those with degrees and several years' experience are qualified to take the National Council for Interior Design Qualification (NCDIQ) certification examination. The NCDIQ is a six-part test that measures all of the above skills. Certified designers generally belong to prestigious design organizations, obtain licenses, and use their certification as a professional reference.

Designers usually receive one to three years of on-the-job training. Experienced professionals make an average of $30,000 a year, although that can vary greatly. Method of payment can be almost as creative as the field itself: Billing can be by the hour ($50 and up), the square foot ($3 to $5 per), on a retail basis (receiving the difference between actual cost and the sticker price), as well as 15 to 40 percent of the wholesale cost, or a combination. Most designers require a retainer fee before drawing up preliminary plans.

Initial presentations include furniture layout, fabric and product recommendations, as well as suggestions for color, lighting, and use of space. Some designers also place orders and supervise labor and installation.

Employment can be found in design and architectural firms, department and home furnishing stores, and in hotel and restaurant chains. In addition to the regular start-up expenses, designers striking out on their own should have exceptionally attractive office spaces, giving clients a preview of the delights to come.

Associations

American Society of Interior Designers
608 Massachusetts Ave., NE
Washington, DC 20002
202/546-3480

Foundation for Interior Design Education Research
60 Monroe Center
Grand Rapids, MI 49503
616/458-0400

Interior Design Educators Council
14252 Culver Drive, Suite A-311
Irvine, CA 92714
714/551-1622

International Society of Interior Designers
433 S. Spring Street, 10th Floor
Los Angeles, CA 90013
213/680-4240

Books

Decorative Style. Embree, James C., et al. New York: Simon and Schuster, 1990.

How to Make Your Design Business Profitable. Stewart, Joyce M. Cincinnati: North Light, 1992.

Human Factors in Industrial Design. Burgess, John H. Blue Ridge Summit, PA: TAB, 1989.
Interior Design Reference Manual. Ballast, David D. Belmont, CA: Professional Publications, nd.
The Measure of Man and Woman. Tilley, Alvin R. New York: Whitney Library of Design, 1993.

Magazines

Contract Design
Hospitality Design
Interior Design
Interiors

Nancy Hoff Barsotti
Commercial Interior Designer

In her nearly twenty-five years as a designer, Nancy Hoff Barsotti of Pittsburgh, Pennsylvania has decorated residences and businesses, including retail stores, stadium boxes, doctor's offices—even a bomb shelter. "You need to understand the company, what they do, and the image they're trying to convey," she observes. "How many employees do they have? Do clients visit them or is most of the work done by phone? How do they want to utilize corporate colors, logo, and pictures of products?"

The bottom line should be worked out during the initial contact. "Get an idea of their budget and deadline for the project. Parameters should be set as early as possible so you know your limits."

Now comes her favorite part: "taking ideas and pulling them all together. I try to do something different, to enhance the work space in a way unique to the company's personality." If the honchos in charge like the proposal—and most decisions in corporations are made by committee —she goes ahead and works out the final details, such as ordering furniture and accessories.

According to Hoff Barsotti, getting clients is the toughest part of the job. "In this business, there's no room for amateurs," she states. "Companies are downsizing, and no one wants to be a guinea pig. Certain basic skills are required, even of someone just starting out."

Jewelry Appraiser

How exciting to work around some of the most beautiful and expensive objects in the world, to handle them and admire their artistry and be exposed to those who wear or confiscate them. Gems and jewelry are evaluated for purchase, liquidation, estates, loan collateral, and insurance replacement purposes, with information reported and conveyed in a recognized and precise language. Such is the life of the jewelry appraiser.

But what they don't tell you is that to get there—at least the right way—you'll need several thousand dollars to become both a certified gemologist and a competent appraiser, as well as several thousand more to obtain the equipment (microscope, spectroscope, refractometer, polariscope, and others) to set up business.

Along with good color vision, writing skills, a high degree of accuracy, and the proper contacts, you must be able to discern the fakes from the real thing and set a fair market value. And with today's technology and laboratory-grown gemstones, it's easy to be deceived unless you know what you're doing. Professional appraisers are liable in court for their actions.

Most appraisers start elsewhere in the jewelry business, either in retail or wholesale, or even in manufacturing and design. They can receive the graduate gemologist degree from the Gemological Institute of America (GIA), a multifaceted organization that offers on-campus classes in the United States and abroad as well as learn-at-home and extension courses.

Along with furnishing some tools, the classes—which can take from several months to a few years, depending on your schedule—emphasize diamond grading and testing; identification of synthetic and natural colored stones; determining color, clarity, and cut; and other information. You also learn how to handle stones without destroying them, always a good idea when dealing with thousands of dollars' worth of other people's merchandise.

The appraising part involves adhering to the *Uniform Standards of Professional Appraisal Practice*, a twenty-eight-page document that sets forth ethical considerations in evaluating properties and is required by the government, institutions, and corporations. The American Society of Appraisers and the International Society of Appraisers (see below) provide certification courses and testing in this area and can help beginning appraisers.

There are only about one thousand fully trained jewelry appraisers in the United States. And unless you own your own business or have another sideline, pay is in the mid-$20,000-a-year range. But if you're good, clients will know they've found a real gem.

Associations

American Society of Appraisers
Box 17265
Washington, DC 20041
800/272-8258

Gemological Institute of America
1660 Stewart Street
Santa Monica, CA 90404
800/421-7250

International Society of Appraisers
P.O. Box 726
Hoffman Estates, IL 60195
708/882-0706

Jewelers of America
1185 Avenue of the Americas
New York, NY 10036
212/768-8777

National Association of Jewelry Appraisers
P.O. Box 6558
Annapolis, MD 21401
301/261-8270

Books

Gems and Jewelry Appraising. Miller, Anna M. New York: Van Nostrand Reinhold, 1988.
Illustrated Guide to Jewelry Appraising. Miller, Anna M. New York: Van Nostrand Reinhold, 1989.
The Professional's Guide of Jewelry Insurance Appraising. Geolat, Patti J., et al. Lincolnshire, IL: Advance, 1994.

Magazines

GEM Correspondent
Modern Jeweler
Jewelers Circular Keystone
Jewelry Appraiser
Personal Property Journal

Larry Phillips
Intinerant Appraiser

Larry Phillips of Albuquerque, New Mexico travels around the United States with his portable lab and laptop computer, writing appraisals for federal marshals, the wealthy, bank trust departments, and lawyers. He sees himself as a sort of rolling detective, uncovering the mysteries behind a particular piece. "There's no such thing as a simple appraisal," he observes. A graduate of the GIA, he has received certification and has many years' experience.

Along with identifying the stone, he must determine qualitative ranking (how it compares to others of its ilk) and condition as well as take into consideration what the market will bear and the purpose of the appraisal. "You begin with a lot of phone calls and contacts to get an idea of what's going on out there. Dollar values may also vary, say, if it's being insured rather than sold."

It perturbs Phillips that so many so-called appraisers are improperly educated. "They can afford to work cheap because they don't have the equipment or take the time or do the research. Over the past fifteen to twenty years, there's been an entirely new body of knowledge on how to set the value of items. Certain things about an appraisal must be consistent, whether you're dealing with a diamond, a backhoe, or a Rembrandt."

Tattoo Artist

Like the ink injected into your skin, tattooing is here to stay and, in fact, has been around since Biblical times. But there are few actual instructional guides on the tattooing process. People learn through an apprenticeship of several years.

This is not a job for those with an aversion to needles. Basically, tattooing involves first swabbing the selected body part with alcohol and then marking the pattern with a stencil. Large numbers of designs are available on sheets of "flash," artist-generated renderings that decorate just about every available surface of the tattoo studio.

Then the real fun begins. You, the tattoo artist, pierce small, deep holes into your customer's skin with a tattoo pen, a high speed vibrating needle that etches out the pattern and injects pigments. This can be tricky: Not only are there different-sized needles for various purposes (narrow ones draw lines, wider ones shade in surfaces and colors) but not all colors react the same with the epidermis. For instance, blue and red pigments produce purple on some types of skin and brown on others. So along with the ability to draw, you need to understand skin texture, muscle tension, pigmentation, anatomy, and chemistry.

Most apprentices are reluctant to administer a tattoo. Instead, they closely observe the experienced artist and assist in the shop, cleaning, gathering needles, and sterilizing. They also learn how to fix mistakes, since most tattoos retain their full color and clarity for about a decade.

Those who work in a tattoo shop can purchase a pen, which costs between three to four hundred dollars. Others who want to start their own studio should be prepared to invest about ten thousand dollars over and above the usual rental, insurance, and overhead for such specialty items as a sterilizer, needles, and pigment.

Prices average from $50 to $100 per tattoo, depending on geographical area and the fame of the artist. Those who build a good reputation can expect to make a decent and steady living. Those skilled at freehand drawing may do even better, for tattoos are as varied as the individuals who wear them.

Associations

Captain's Cove Seaport (formerly Tattoo Club of America)
c/o Spider Webb's Studios
1 Bostwick Ave.
Bridgeport, CT 06605
203/335-3992

National Tattoo Association (formerly National Tattoo Club of the World)
465 Business Park Lane
Allentown, PA 18103-9120
215/433-7261

Professional Tattoo Artists Guild/
Empire State Tattoo Club of America
P.O. Box 1374
Mt. Vernon, NY 10550
914/664-9894

Books

Art, Sex, and Symbol. Scutt, R. W. B. New York: Cornwall Books, 1986.

Tattooing A to Z. Spaulding, Huck. Vorheesville, NY: Spaulding and Rogers, 1988.

Magazines

The Tattoo Advocate Journal
Tattootime
Skin Art
Tattoo

Lyle Tuttle
Tattoo Artist

When Lyle Tuttle was 14, he hopped aboard a Greyhound bus to San Francisco and got his first tattoo. That was in 1947, and he's been involved with tattoos ever since. Not only does he have his own studio in San Francisco but he owns one of the world's largest collections of tattoo memorabilia.

"Tattoo artists should be conscientious and aware of health and cleanliness," Tuttle observes. "Otherwise everyone involved could become exposed to communicable diseases." Training is also very important: "Pay close attention to how things are done, then develop your own style."

Although tattooing's not for everyone (obviously), Tuttle says, "Those who enjoy giving and wearing tattoos are often the most motivated to succeed, even if they don't have as much artistic talent. They persist and teach themselves." Some catch on quickly, while others can apprentice at a tattoo studio for years, "and never quite meet the profession's exacting standards."

According to Tuttle, tattoo artists spend as much time learning their craft as dentists. One big difference, though: most of the former don't drive BMWs.

Window Merchandiser

Although a few art schools offer degrees in window, or visual, merchandising, most people in this occupation either train abroad or are self-taught. Along with having a good sense of color, lighting, and arrangement, you need to be handy with props, needle and thread, paint brush and paints, and hammer and nails. The window, showcase, or point-of-purchase display is entirely your responsibility from conception to teardown.

You must be persistent, because most of your clients will be smaller boutiques, stores, and travel agencies that can't afford to hire full-time display help. Companies, too, may occasionally need displays, especially for trade shows, or if they're remodeling or building new offices. Along with the usual phone calls and brochures, you can drop by and talk to the manager, showing him or her photographs of your work and emphasizing how you'll make the merchandise more appealing. Anything can be effectively arranged, be it washers and dryers, tools, or evening gowns.

Window dressers understand the principles of display. They know the importance of balance and proportion, how to create mood and setting, how to use color (i.e., green works with springtime scenes), and have an awareness of what the product and customers are about. They also know how to construct and disassemble sets. Most displays must be erected in a day; the longer a window is "down," the fewer customers see the product.

Of course, much more time is required in actual planning. The trick is to be organized and have as much done as possible before actual setup. Professionals do not intrude on the regular work flow, are careful with merchandise, and are thorough with cleanup.

You must also work closely with clients, making sure they understand every step of the design process as well as the end result. They should have a good idea of the expenses and time involved before the project begins. Beginners in this field make only about $7 to $9 per hour; successful and experienced window designers can realize an annual income in the mid-$30,000s.

Start-up costs can be steep, considering that you must furnish a basic line of props. These can run from silk flowers to columns, to vases, to mannequins. However, you can also be imaginative and save money by buying secondhand items and making them look glamorous.

Window merchandising is more about group psychology than individual taste. Your personal vision may not jive with what draws customers to the store, but if the result is increased sales, you've created your own window of opportunity.

Associations

American Society of Interior Designers
60B Massachusetts, Ave., NE
Washington, DC 20002
202/546-3480

Foundation for Interior Design Education Research
60 Monroe Center
Grand Rapids, MI 49503
616/458-0400

Interior Design Educators Council
14252 Culver Drive, Suite A-311
Irvine, CA 92714
714/551-1622

International Society of Interior Designers
433 S. Spring Street, 10th Floor
Los Angeles, CA 90013
213/680-4240

Books

Applied Visual Merchandising. Mills, Kenneth and Judith Paul. Englewood Cliffs, NJ: Prentice-Hall, 1988.

Display Design. Roth, Laszlo. New York: Prentice-Hall, 1983.

How To Display It. Foster, Eric and Trudy Ralston. New York: Art Direction, 1985.

How To Understand and Use Display. Hattori, Harushisa. Tokyo, Japan: Graphic-sha, 1988.

Visual Merchandising and Display. Pegler, Martin. New York: Fairchild, 1983.

Magazines

General Merchandise News
Inside Retailing
Retailing Today
Store Planning
Views
Visual Merchandising & Store Design

Ursula Schluter
Window Merchandiser

Although she trained in Europe, Ursula Schluter of Edmunds, Washington, takes an Americanized approach, designing spaces of different sizes and shapes. "I work for large companies and little stores," she says. These include women's apparel retailers along with companies that sell hard-line merchandise such as computer equipment.

Schluter first develops a concept of how to portray the item, then purchases or builds the necessary props. "The idea is to create a mood and a setting. For instance, I structure a towel display around a luxurious Roman bath." She cautions beginning designers to "build in" the time it takes to conceptualize and organize the display. "Otherwise you might shortchange yourself or have to redo your estimate."

Although Schluter's goal is to evoke customer response, "You can't win everybody," she explains. "If the display appeals to 50 percent of the people you're doing well."

To err is human, but to really foul things up requires a computer.

—ANONYMOUS

Computer Wizards

Computer Consultant/Doctor
Desktop Publisher
Manual Tester/Writer
Software Designer

Computer Consultant/Doctor

At $100 and more an hour, these folks can make as much as their medical counterparts. And they don't have to worry about being sued by their patients. But computer consultants must have an intimate, working knowledge of the customer's system that no one else has. And therein lies the catch: With all the hardware and software out there, where do you begin?

Most start out with PC (desktop) and local area network (LAN) computers. They deal with small and medium-sized businesses and popular applications such as MS-DOS or Windows. These systems are in demand, fairly standard, and easy to set up and maintain, thus allowing for a high volume of customers. You'll need a background in one or two programming languages and knowledge of a hardware platform (that is, IBM or its clones). At this level, you can charge $35 to $75 an hour.

Consultants with broader skills know several different programming languages, are familiar with computer aided software engineering (CASE) technology, and can not only develop new information systems but can integrate new components with old ones. They handle the transitions among different technologies and work with PCs, small systems, and mainframes. At this level, $75 to $150 an hour is a realistic fee.

Experts in database management systems, artificial intelligence, technology planning, multilevel database security, and other specific areas are in the stratosphere of consulting. They travel around the world, providing specialized skills to corporations that invest millions of dollars in computers. Like superstar M.D.s, they can write their own ticket. But these jobs are few indeed.

As a consultant, you'll need to address the client's needs. This involves understanding and speaking the jargon of his or her business while keeping computerese to a minimum, and then proposing a realistic, low-cost application. The client may be getting a "second opinion" from a rival consultant, so it's in your best interest to stay as competitive as possible. Along with personal characteristics such as congeniality, integrity, and problem-solving skills, you'll need to demonstrate in-depth knowledge of hardware and software as well as programming and trouble-shooting ability.

There are literally dozens of consulting possibilities. These range from designing applications for small and medium-sized businesses to overseeing hardware and software maintenance, to conducting training and education, to serving as a security specialist who prevents computer viruses. A background in computer science, business, and even accounting will add to your skills. Keeping up with trends is also important in determining the direction to steer your business.

Even the most technology-phobic companies are beginning to understand the need for a computer-literate adviser with specialized skills. An on-call person who saves them the trouble of hiring a full-time expert and makes the "durn things" work can be invaluable. But before making that first visit, be familiar with the client's dress code. And those who wear pocket protectors should probably leave them at home.

Associations

Independent Computer Consultants Association
933 Gardenview Office Parkway
St. Louis, MO 63141
800-438-4222

National Association of Computer Consulting Businesses
1250 Connecticut Ave., NW, Suite 700
Washington, DC 20036
202/637-6483

Books

Computer Troubleshooting and Maintenance. McBride, Walter J. San Diego: Harcourt Brace Jovanovich, 1988.

The Computer Consultant's Guide. Ruhl, Janet. New York: Wiley, 1994.

High-Tech Consulting. Zarrella, John. Suisun City, CA: Microcomputer Applications, nd.

How To Be a Successful Computer Consultant. Simon, Alan R. New York: McGraw-Hill, 1994.

Rookie Trouble-Shooting. Dunning, Jack, et al. San Diego: Computer Publishing Enterprises, 1993.

Magazines

Computer and Information Systems Abstracts
Consultation Abstracts

Beyond Computing
Database Review
Computerworld
Wired

Rich Evans
Computer Doctor

Rich Evans of Garden Grove, California, finds that most of his customers' difficulties are those of interpretation and can be solved by the user's manual. "That saves them the expense of having me come out," he observes. The rest is "primarily incompatibility between different releases in the software and an upgraded system. It's not a question of a problem, but whether there really is one. You apply logic to get to the heart of the matter and isolate where the trouble is."

Over the last fifteen years, Evans has seen a tremendous improvement in computers. "Equipment reliability has increased tenfold, particularly in the Hewlett-Packard," the hardware he works with. The downside, of course, is that there's less need for "doctoring." "The systems test themselves and will call the vendor's computer at 4 A.M. and report an error before users even know about it."

Still, networks and applications have become increasingly complicated and, according to Evans, "companies can look at hundreds of options instead of just ten or fifteen. I can tailor-make a program to best fit their needs, even setting up a communications system among previously incompatible networks." He also offers training classes in database management: "Many times I 'give' my doctoring skills away as part of the bid process. I may lose a few dollars in the short run, but get a long-term customer."

Desktop Publisher

Even in the fast-paced world of computers, this is the new kid on the block. Desktop publishing (DTP) didn't really exist until 1985, when Paul Brainerd, then president of Seattle's Aldus Corporation, developed the PageMaker program for Macintosh computers. IBM-style applications soon followed, and a cottage industry generating its own illustrated brochures, books, magazines, color slides, newsletters, and other printed matter was born. Drawing programs, scanners, clip art from CD-ROMs, and other software with thousands of typefaces and fonts can aid in the professional production of just about any written material.

But the new can be risky, and those interested in this field should start with basic equipment (a computer with room for expansion, a color monitor, and an inexpensive letter-quality printer) before investing thousands of dollars in additional memory, laser printers, a CD-ROM, and specialized programs. You can purchase a decent setup for about fifteen hundred dollars.

Computer literacy is necessary, as you will be learning and working with many types of programs and accoutrements to get the job done. Classes and seminars at computer stores and through associations (see below) are useful, although sometimes it's best just to sit down with the instructional manual and go through the program yourself. You should also be familiar with word processing.

Desktop publishers should know basic layout and design, including graphics, pasteup, and typography. Training is available at community colleges, although the information and equipment they offer may lag behind the technology.

The meshing of DTP and the printing industry hasn't always been smooth. Traditional printers feel (and perhaps rightfully so) that upstart desktop publishers have "stolen" from their client base and created work that is less than professional looking. Many printers still believe nothing replaces traditional typesetting, although with the advancement of technology, computer-generated and offset-press material are becoming indistinguishable. Already, some desktop publishers can output their product to film, bypassing much of the regular printing process. This saves money and time while preserving the quality of work.

A desktop publisher who provides clients with a mock-up before going to press, meets deadlines, and creates high-caliber publications more cheaply than a standard print shop can pull in from $55,000 to $80,000 a year. Customers can range from a Fortune 500 company wanting to produce a four-color annual report to someone looking to self-publish his grandmother's memoirs. But it's best to keep abreast of the latest developments or a competitor might pull the plug on your business.

Associations

Association for the Development of Electronic Publishing Techniques
360 N. Michigan Ave.
Chicago, IL 60601
312/609-0577

Association for Desktop Publishers
P.O. Box 881667
San Diego, CA 92168
619/563-7914

National Association for Desktop Publishers
Museum Wharf
300 Congress St.
Boston, MA
617/426-2885

Books

The Art of Desktop Publishing. Bove, Tony, et al. New York: Bantam, 1990.

Careers in Word Processing and Desktop Publishing. Spencer, Jean. New York: Rosen, 1990.
Desktop Publishers Survival Kit. Blatner, David. Berkeley, CA: Peachpit Press, 1992.
Desktop Publishing by Design. Shushan, Ronnie. Redmond, WA: Microsoft, 1991.
Opportunities in Desktop Publishing Careers. Schiff, Kenny. Lincolnwood, IL: NTC, 1993.

Magazines

Desktop Communications
Desktop Publisher
PC Publishing
Personal Publishing
Publish
many others

Tracy Lundy
Desktop Publisher

Lundy Associates of Lake Forest, California, is equipped to create everything "from flyers to sales presentations to slides to directories," says owner Tracy Lundy. "I also provide word processing and do large scan jobs, such as contracts and scripts for a Hollywood producer."

Although Lundy started modestly, she now has both IBM and Macintosh equipment, conversion programs, CD-ROM, a color scanner, sophisticated printers and software, and lots of memory "because the programs are getting so big."

She has kept many of the same clients since 1988 when she first opened the business. "I never say no and don't charge a premium. I believe in going that extra mile."

Manual Tester/Writer

Someone hands you a computer disk and tells you to start running the program. Now you're really confused.

That's where software manual testers and writers come in. Without lucid instructions and dependable applications, even the best program is meaningless to the average computer user. So along with producing effective documentation, testers/writers run through the entire program, checking for "bugs" and inconsistencies. So, in addition to knowledge of computers, writing and communications skills are a must. College classes in these subjects as well as in English and editing are helpful as is previous experience in the computer industry.

As a manual tester/writer, you may be called in during product development to create initial documentation or edit something that's poorly written. If you're starting from scratch, you'll need to find out the type of publication your client wants. It can be a *tutorial*, which teaches basic functions through controlled practice sessions; a *procedures guide*, which explains and provides step-by-step instructions; a *reference material*, which details commands, functions, fields, key assignments, and messages; a *quick reference* card or template, which lists the most frequently used of the previous items; or *online help system* screen displays, which provide instructions. Companies often ask for more than one of these categories.

You'll also be responsible for layout and illustrations. The latter are important to users in understanding the program because many don't have the patience or desire to ponder your carefully crafted words. Captions, pictures, or "dumps" (actual depictions of the computer screen), diagrams and drawings, charts, tables, icons (especially with Windows applications), and even photographs for a hardware installation can make or break an effective manual. And the writing must be clear and concise, with effective use of lists and short paragraphs. This is not the place for a budding James Joyce.

Testers/writers assigned to "rescue" a rough-draft version flag and fix difficult sections, correct inaccurate information, misleading artwork, and poor organization. They rewrite and redesign problem areas, making sure the entire manual flows smoothly and is easy to follow.

Often editing jobs are last minute and under tight deadlines since the manual can be an afterthought to production. But with a basic computer setup, you can pull in a cool $30 to $50 an hour. And the next time the company may call you and have you pen the whole thing.

Associations

American Software Association
1616 N. Ft. Meyer Street
Arlington, VA 22209
703/522-5055

Society for Software Quality
P.O. Box 86958
San Diego, CA 92138
619/297-1544

Software Management Association
P.O. Box 120004
Vallejo, CA 94590
707/643-4423

Books

The Computer Professional's Guide to Effective Communication. Simon, Alan R. New York: McGraw-Hill, 1993.
How to Write a Really Good User's Manual. Katzin, Emanuel. New York: Van Nostrand Reinhold, 1985.
Writing Better Computer User Documentation. Brockmann, R. John. New York: Wiley, 1986.

Writing Effective Software Documentation. Williams, Patricia and Pamela Beason. Glenview, IL: Scott, Foresman, 1990.

Magazines

Acronyms
Advances in Engineering
Computeriter
Computer Software News
Computers & Composition
Technical Communications Journal

Bobbie Belanger
Software Manual Writer

Before branching out on her own, Bobbie Belanger of San Pedro, California, worked with computers in a corporate setting for over thirty years. Now semiretired, she has one client who keeps her busy. "There's a real need for someone who can interpret technical and obscure applications for everyday users," she observes. "It's not as easy as it appears, because you have to understand exactly what the program is about."

Those who find themselves being called by friends and asked to decipher computerese may have a knack for this field. "But you need to be able to explain it over the phone, rather than come over and demonstrate."

More companies are turning from printed matter toward online tutorials. "With the advent of CD-ROMs, it's simpler to put the CD in the drive and look it up. Manuals are smaller and often direct users toward online help."

But there will always be a need for clearly written instructions. "As programs become more complex, the challenge lies in determining how to make it easier for the user."

Software Designer

The only shade of gray in this job is the matter inside your head. You really need to know your stuff, including several different program languages (COBOL, FORTRAN, ASCII) or artificial intelligence or object-oriented languages (Prolog, LISP, C++) as well as hardware and operating systems and other computer building blocks. You then process this knowledge into working solutions for clients. And a two or, more commonly, four-year degree in computer science and information systems management isn't enough—operational and business skills, marketing analysis, research ability, and a love of logic and mystery also come into play. But your output can reap great financial and professional rewards.

Basically, software designers go into businesses and find out how to best automate operations, be they inventory levels, financial records, personnel files, or even the temperature in office buildings. The software varies with the type of information generated, with the different requirements for, say, updating invoices or programming a flight simulator.

You assess needs, create a chart showing how the program will work, and determine the components that will appear on each screen. Then, based on the customer's existing equipment or preferences, you come up with compatible software. Each step is broken down into a logical series of instructions and is coded into the language the computer can follow.

This can take a few weeks or much longer, with the client being consulted and giving approval during every phase of development. Before being put into use, the new program is "debugged" by preparing sample tasks that test all components. After reviewing the results, any errors are eliminated through revision and additional testing. If you've created something good, you can market it elsewhere as long as you've written it on your own equipment or have paid the clients for use of their computer.

Software designers also update, repair, and modify existing programs. They can do this manually, inserting comments in the coded instructions so users can understand the changes, or through computer-aided software engineering, which automates some of the basic processes.

Designers can work in *applications*, which deals with creating or revising programs for specific jobs. Or they can focus on *systems*, maintaining the software that controls the operation of an entire computer system, and making changes on how the central processing unit and peripherals (terminals, printers, drives) handle jobs.

Given the popularity and increasing general use of computers, and the fact that much of what software designers do is still a mystery to the rest of us, they will continue to be in demand. An average salary is about $36,000, and often more, for independent operators.

Associations

Association for Computing Machinery
1515 Broadway
New York, NY 10036
212/869-7440

Institute for Certification of Computer Professionals
220 E. Devon Ave., Suite 268
Des Plaines, IL 60018
708/299-4227

Books

The Healthy Software Project. Norris, Mark, et al. New York: Wiley, 1990.

The Other Side of Software. Shamlin, Carolyn. New York: AMACOM, 1990.

Software Requirements. Davis, Alan M. Englewood Cliffs, NJ: Prentice-Hall, 1990

Software System Development, A Gentle Introduction. Britton, Carol and Jill Doake. London: McGraw-Hill International, 1993.

Software That Works. Ward, Michael. San Diego: Academic, 1990.

Magazines

Advances in Software Sciences and Technology
Computer Design
Computer Technology Review
Design Automation
Software Critique
Software Journal
many others

Ed Rosen
Applications Designer

"It's important to be flexible," observes Ed Rosen, owner of Data Bank Associates, a Germantown, Maryland, enterprise that makes a range of software products for computer companies and international organizations. "Today's consumers have a lot to choose from, so you need a broad base of knowledge."

Clarity is also essential. "The product must be well-written and intuitive, so it makes sense to users." Consideration of the marketplace is yet another factor: "Each nation has its own set of cultural references" says Rosen. If you're creating software for multinational use, each term must be expressed in the right context."

Programming requires a heavy initial investment of time and effort. "The primary development phase is the most difficult and expensive. So when you're out there in the real world you need to factor it into your cost."

The only reason I would take up jogging is so I could hear heavy breathing again.

—ERMA BOMBECK

Fit and Healthy

Diet Consultant
Fitness Instructor
Massage Therapist
Midwife
Personal Trainer
Traveling Nurse

Diet Consultant

According to government studies, thirty-four million adult Americans are considered obese and approximately fifty million are dieting at any given time. There's a fair amount of money to be made in the weight-loss industry, and several different types of jobs are available in this field. The most expensive (in terms of education) but ultimately rewarding is that of registered dietician (RD), or nutritionist. This involves either a specialized four-year program that combines academic and practical experience or an undergraduate degree that also meets American Dietetic Association requirements and includes an additional nine hundred hours of supervised work. Students take courses in foods, nutrition, and chemistry, along with business, mathematics, statistics, computer science, biology, and other sciences. Internships and graduate programs are also available.

As a nutritionist, you'll plan programs and supervise meals, help prevent and treat illnesses by promoting good eating habits, evaluate clients' diets, and suggest modifications according to their health needs, among many other things. Jobs are available in hospitals, clinics (public and private), institutions, and companies, and can range from developing menus for a school cafeteria to analyzing the impact of a company's products and nutrition labeling. You can also set up your own practice, provided you are an RD and have had one to four years of clinical and community experience. Depending upon background and type of position, salaries vary from $28,000 to $40,000—possibly even more for independent RDs with large followings.

Or you can opt to become a dietetic technician. These jobs require an associate arts degree and 450 hours of supervised experience. With less intensive training in nutrition care and foods, you'll be a second banana, so to speak, assisting the nutritionist. But you get to conduct patient interviews, help choose proper foods, arrange meal plans, provide input in preparing educational materials, and more. Pay is in the $20,000 range, give or take a few grand.

Perhaps the easiest entrée into this burgeoning arena is employment at a weight-loss company, such as Weight Watchers, Jenny Craig, or Optifast. With little formal training, you basically "sell" the program to customers, motivating and encouraging them to stay with their weight-loss efforts and buy the products. This requires empathy and patience, since people become discouraged when they "plateau" at a certain weight and are faced with temptation from family and friends. If it's a program you believe in, and you work on commission and draw in lots of clients, you can make between $20,000 and $30,000 a year.

These jobs are flexible because many positions are part-time and turnover can be high.

Make sure the company you go to work for is reliable and not being investigated by the Federal Trade Commission for false advertising as was Nutri/System before it closed a few years ago. And if someone comes up with a miracle cure for obesity, plan on collecting unemployment.

Associations

American Association of Nutritional Consultants
1641 E. Sunset Blvd.
Las Vegas, NE 89119
702/361-1132

American College of Nutrition
301 East 17th Street
New York, NY 10003
212/777-1037

American Dietetic Association
216 W. Jackson Blvd., Suite 800
Chicago, IL 60606-6995
312/899-0400

American Institute of Nutrition
9650 Rockville Pike
Bethesda, MD 20814
301/530-7050

Society for Nutrition Education
2001 Killebrew, Suite 340
Minneapolis, MN 55425
612/854-0035

Books

Exploring Careers in Dietetics and Nutrition. Kane, June K. New York: Rosen, 1987.

Handbook of Clinical Nutrition. Weinsier, Roland L. St. Louis: Mosby, 1981.

Nutrition. Smolin, Lori and M. Grosvenor. Fort Worth, TX: Saunders, 1994.

Nutrition and Living Today and Tomorrow. Pond, Wilson. Danville, IL: Interstate, 1989.

Opportunities in Nutrition Careers. Caldwell, Carol C. Lincolnwood, IL: NTC, 1992.

Magazines

Contemporary Nutrition
Food, Nutrition, & Health
Food and Nutrition Magazine
Food and Nutrition News
Health, Diet and Nutrition
Nutrition Counselor
Nutrition Today
many others

Debbie Cornwell
Weight-Loss Counselor

When Debbie Cornwell of Atlanta, Georgia, met a woman who'd had successful results with the Jenny Craig program, she knew she'd found her new vocation. "I come from a retail management background and wanted to help people," she recalls. "I also like being my own boss, without the pressure of owning a business."

The job involves more than encouraging customers to lose weight. "We are provided with in-depth training about the program and how to handle clients. Then, each month, we have continuing education classes about a specific aspect of weight loss, such as encouraging adolescents and maintenance.

"You must also be able to deal with the public, which means all kinds of situations," she adds. Sometimes she finds herself in the middle of a juggling act—taking a phone call from someone who wants to know everything about the program while holding a counseling session with a customer. "You need to be calm and upbeat and make the client feel like he's the most important."

Fitness Instructor

Although they look glamorous with their leotards and body parts of steel, fitness instructors need more than enthusiasm, muscle tone, and a loud voice. CPR certification, along with training in health and physical education; exercise physiology; choreography; voice projection and cueing; kinesiology and biomechanics; basic anatomy and injury prevention; even nutrition and body composition are the basic requirements for this field. Some courses are taught at colleges, while others are available only through certifying associations (starred below).

And you need to decide whether you want to be an independent contractor, work for an existing organization such as Jazzercise, or be retained by a health club or corporation. Remuneration can vary from $9 to $30 an hour or can be on a sliding scale according to the number of clients you attract.

If self-employed instructors develop a large following, they can make a good profit. But they must meet the overhead—renting space; providing music, equipment, and personal exercise clothes; purchasing liability insurance; and other costs. Start-up expenses alone can be a couple of thousand dollars or more.

Those hired by organizations such as Jazzercise are periodically provided with music and choreography, as well as with some clothing. Like independents, however, they'll need to locate their own venue, be it a church, school, dance studio, or nursing home. The purchase of the franchise covers many costs.

Instructors working at health clubs often create their own routines, but may find themselves answering phones, cleaning up the facility, and pitching memberships to potential clients as well. So it's best to know what the duties are before signing on.

Traveling instructors can fly to various cities as representatives of their employer or work on a cruise ship (see Cruise Worker) or at a resort. Salaries may be slightly less, but room, board, and transportation are paid for.

You may want to focus on a certain specialty: low, medium, or high impact classes; slideaerobics; stepaerobics; aquacize; the pregnant; the overweight; seniors; or those with special needs. You must also know how to handle a "mixed" gathering consisting of different levels of fitness. Along with understanding the limitations of each group, make sure the clients do the routines correctly while working to their fullest potential. Training helps avoid possible lawsuits and injury.

Fitness instructors should monitor their own activities as well, taking on no more than fifteen classes a week. Nothing mangles a promising career like a shin splint or torn muscle.

Associations

Aerobics Center*
12200 Preston Road
Dallas, TX 75230
214/239-7223

Aerobics and Fitness Association of America (AFFA)*
15250 Ventura Blvd., Suite 200
Sherman Oaks, CA 91403
800/225-2322

American College of Sports Medicine*
P.O. Box 1440
Indianapolis, IN 46206
317/637-9200

American Council on Exercise*
Exer-Safety Association
P.O. Box 391466
Solon, OH 44139
216/562-8280

International Dance-Exercise Association (IDDEA)
6190 Cornerstone Court E., Suite 204
San Diego, CA 92121
619/535-8979

*These associations offer certification.

Books

Aerobic Dance. Mazzeo, Karen and Judy Kisselle. Englewood, CO: Morton, 1987.

Fitness and Wellness. Hoeger, Werner. Englewood, CO Morton, 1990.

Leading Aerobic Dance-Exercise. Wilmoth, Susan K. Champaign, IL: Human Kinetics, 1986.

Opportunities in Fitness Careers. Rosenbaum, Jean and Mary Miller. Lincolnwood IL: NTC, 1991.

Magazines

Aerobic Beat
Aerobics News
American Fitness
Fitness Bulletin
Fitness Management
Women's Sports and Fitness

Traci Freeman
AFFA Instructor

"Today most employers and clients want a certified instructor, regardless of level of education," observes Traci Freeman of Sherman Oaks, California. But before taking the certification test, you need to have some experience, preferably under the supervision of another certified instructor.

Freeman teaches classes that emphasize floor work and utilize various muscle groups. "I choreograph my own moves and try to push people beyond what they think their limits are." But they know what they're getting into beforehand and are motivated.

She has an open-door policy and explains everything to the class. "I tell them what body area they're working and demonstrate the proper technique. I encourage their questions and love helping them make a positive change."

Massage Therapist

In the past, people who went for a "massage" may have been flirting with divorce and venereal disease. But the recent resurgence of holistic health with its appreciation of the healing power of herbs and oils has given this profession long-overdue respect. Usually licensed or certified by their home state, massage therapists take intensive training in anatomy, physiology, and theory. They attend schools or institutes, which usually charge an arm and a leg (about five thousand dollars, give or take a few hundred dollars). Working with oils, or aromatherapy, is an additional area of study. Massage therapy involves a lot more than giving a good backrub.

As the oldest known healing art, massage works on physical, mental, and even spiritual levels, and is often seen as a means of getting in touch with repressed emotions or memories. It also reduces stress and isn't fattening, which explains why it's become so popular. There are many different types of massage: gentle relaxation; firm; neuromuscular, which focuses on trigger points; even specialized massages that relieve common ailments (tension headaches, PMS, water retention) and sports-related and other injuries.

In preparing for the client, the therapist must make sure the environment is soothing. The room should be warmed and painted in pastels, and should have lots of luxurious towels and pillows as well as soothing music and soft lighting. As a therapist, you need to be relaxed as well; you'll be walking in on a total stranger who's partially or completely undressed (though covered with a towel).

After discerning the individual's physical limitations and preferences, you begin, first choosing an essential oil whose fragrance and properties seem to best suit the client's needs. The massage lasts anywhere from thirty minutes to an hour and a half, depending upon your prearranged agreement. After it's completed, allow the client to lie on the table for a few minutes, then note his or her reaction to the massage.

Experienced therapists charge $40 to $50 an hour, or more if they're in a large urban area. This is physically and mentally demanding work, so it's best to limit massages to no more than twenty-five or so a week. Many therapists work part-time at health clubs, spas, or for chiropractors. Others set up their own businesses, but this can be costly considering that you'll likely need to remodel the space and purchase your own equipment. A massage table alone costs five hundred dollars.

Unlike physical therapy, massages usually aren't covered by insurance, which can greatly reduce your potential client base. So you need to be committed, body and soul.

Associations

American Massage Therapy Association
820 Davis Street, Suite 100
Evanston, IL 60201
708/864-0123

Associated Bodywork and Massage Professionals
P.O. Box 1869
Evergreen, CO 80439
303/674-8478

International Myomassethics Federation
3350 South 2300 East
Salt Lake City, UT 84109
800/338-8950

Books

The Body Reveals. Kurtz, Ron and Dr. Hector Prestera. New York: Harper and Row, 1970.
The Complete Body Massage. Harrold, Fiona. New York: Sterling, 1992.
Massage: A Career at Your Fingertips. Ashley, Martin. Barrytown, NY: Straton Hill, 1992,
The Massage Book. Downing, George. London: Arkana, 1989.
Massage Cures. Dawes, Nigel and Fiona Harrold. Wellingborough, U.K.: Thorsons, 1990.
Massage Techniques. Lawrence D. Baloti. New York: Perigee, 1986.

Magazines

Massage
Massage Handbook
Massage Therapy Journal

Anne Hartley
Licensed Massage Therapist

Anne Hartley of Blacklick, Ohio, was relieved when she found she could attend massage school part-time. "I went one to two days a week for a year, while supporting my family," says this single mother who's originally from England.

One of the hardest things about the job is learning when to keep quiet. "People think they know what they want, even if experience tells you something else will work better. So you need to tactfully suggest it for the next time."

Initially hired by a chiropractor, Hartley is now self-employed and does massages part-time for a country club. "At first, some people are uncomfortable about being undressed, so it's up to me to educate them about the benefits of massage and explain that it can help them where medicines and other therapies have failed."

Midwife

This job has a high road and a low road. The high is the way of certified nurse midwives (CNMs), practitioners in a burgeoning field that promises not only salaries from $40,000 to $80,000 a year, but increased respectability and responsibility.

The second route, lay midwifery, is legal only in certain states. Some formal training is available, but it's mostly done through apprenticeship. Practices and procedures from this ancient art have been passed down through the ages. Lay midwives perform births at home and have neither hospital nor prescription-writing privileges. Since insurance doesn't cover their services, they're often paid by barter.

The future looks brighter for certified nurse-midwives. Along with providing preconception, prenatal, labor and delivery, and postpartum care, these women (and a few men) work with doctors and have the latest scoop on women's medical issues. They can prescribe medication and have immediate access to hospitals or physicians should complications develop. Because of their specialized training, they can provide a level of preventative care and individual attention not found in an everyday medical practice. Many women continue to use nurse-midwives for their gynecological and menopausal checkups.

At this time, in order to become a CNM, you must be a registered nurse. However, this may change as others in the healing professions (for instance, physical therapists) attempt entry into the field. Programs are affiliated with universities; you can opt for either a certificate or master's degree. The former involves nine to twelve months of study and completion of a core curriculum, while a master's degree requires all this and an additional year or two, clinical experience, and possibly the Graduate Record Examination. Upon completion of school, you take the certification exam and are then licensed to practice anywhere in the United States, within the limitations posed by each state.

Nurse-midwives have helped reduce teenage pregnancies, premature births, infant mortality and unnecessary surgeries, such as caesareans. They can work in hospitals, birthing centers, or on their own as private practitioners and serve in an educational capacity for the community. Some also teach, do research, and participate in legislative affairs, helping to shape health care reform policies.

The number of in-hospital births attended by CNMs has increased sevenfold in the last fifteen years. According to statistics from the American College of Nurse-Midwives, by the year 2001, graduate schools will have to triple their output to meet the demand. This may not be good news to doctors and lay midwives, but it seems to have greatly helped women.

Associations

American College of Surgeon-Midwives
1522 K Street, NW, Suite 1000
Washington, DC 20005
202/289-0171

Farm Midwives
The Farm
Summertown, TN 38483
(no phone)

Frontier Nursing Service
Wendover, KY 41775
606/672-2318

Books

The Midwife Challenge. Kitzinger, Shelia, ed. London: Pandora, 1991.

The Psychology of Childbirth. Prince, Joyce. New York: Churchill Livingstone, 1987

Spiritual Midwifery. Gaskin, Ina May. Summertown, TN: The Book Publishing Company, 1990.

Magazines

Birth Gazette
Journal of Nurse-Midwifery
Midwifery Today and Childbirth Education
Special Delivery
Quickening

Susan Nickel
Certified Nurse-Midwife

Susan Nickel of Lenore, North Carolina is employed at a women's health center, as one of a group of CNMs who work closely with several doctors and the local hospital. "We provide care for teens through postmenopausal women," she says. "If anything happens, consultants are two blocks and a fax machine away." Each nurse-midwife has her own patients and is on call twenty-four hours a day. "This can be a hard job for a woman with a family."

Although CNMs have found acceptance in rural areas with sparse population and few MDs, larger cities can pose problems. "Some doctors feel threatened," Nickel admits. They may refuse to recognize the CNM or initiate local legislation to impose limitations on her practice. "Yet what we're doing greatly reduces health care costs in terms of training and services."

Nickel takes a collaborative approach. "We view the health care system as a pyramid, with the nurse practitioners and the family doctors providing the broad base of care. If complications arise, patients are referred to specialists and then to centers where they can get the highest level of treatment. This seems the most efficient method."

Personal Trainer

Imagine spending winters in Palm Beach or on the French Riviera, traveling around with the wealthy, movie stars, or corporate dynamos to exotic locations and bustling metropolises. As a personal trainer, you'll formulate an exercise plan for your client, who is probably in a high-profile, demanding occupation. This intensive one-on-one relationship requires patience, in-depth knowledge, and physical and mental stamina.

Like fitness instructors, personal trainers must have an understanding of anatomy, physiology, and CPR, and are almost always certified by fitness organizations. But they also often have undergraduate or advanced degrees in sports medicine, physical education, or exercise physiology or a nursing or other medical background. Some are former bodybuilders or dancers. Many personal trainers start out in gyms, decide they like working with individuals, and begin attracting their own clientele.

As a personal trainer, you'll spend hours doing a fitness assessment and taking an individual history so you can best understand your client's strengths and weaknesses. You'll also need to obtain medical data (and possibly a doctor's consent) as well as information about daily food intake and exercise habits. Some clients may just want to firm and tone, while others may have a specific weight- and inch-loss goal. Clients may have medical limitations, such as injuries or diseases.

Certain clients will focus on aerobics while others plan to do bodybuilding. You must be able to provide answers to their questions and come up with programs that suit their needs. You may be required to travel with the client so that he or she can maintain the exercise routine. However, the client must be prepared to compensate you accordingly, because most trainers have a base of people with whom they work and usually see three or more clients a day. Because it can be difficult to juggle so many busy schedules, you need to be flexible.

Pay ranges from $25 to $75 an hour, and more for exclusive patrons. Start-up costs can be as little as a few hundred dollars for portable equipment and liability insurance for those who are already certified. You won't likely need a studio because most workouts are held in customers' homes and offices. Some trainers provide consultation services for heath clubs. But you'll be required to tactfully motivate sometimes difficult and demanding clients as well as educate them about their limitations. And in a business that relies almost totally on word-of-mouth, your reputation is often your only advertisement.

Associations

Aerobics Center*
12200 Preston Road
Dallas, TX 75230
214/239-7223

Aerobics and Fitness Association of America*
15250 Ventura Blvd., Suite 200
Sherman Oaks, CA 91403
800/225-2322

American College of Sports Medicine*
P.O. Box 1440
Indianapolis, IN 46206
317/637-9200

American Council on Exercise*
Exer-Safety Association
P.O. Box 391466
Solon, OH 44139
216/562-8280

International Dance-Exercise Association
6190 Cornerstone Court E., Suite 204
San Diego, CA 92121
619/535-8979

*These associations offer certification.

Books

Bases of Fitness. Fox, Edward, et al. New York: Macmillan, 1987.
Exercise Physiology. McArdle, William D., et al. Philadelphia: Lea and Febinger, 1991.
The Personal Trainer Business Book. Gagon, Denis and Lorraine Forrester. Los Angeles: IDEA, 1992
Personal Trainer Manual. Sudy, Mitchell, ed. San Diego: American Council on Exercise, 1991.
Physiology of Fitness. Sharkey, Brian. Champaign: IL: Human Kinetics, 1990.
See also Fitness Instructor

Magazines

Being Well
Exercise & Physical Fitness Programs
Exercise Physiology
See also Fitness Instructor

Patti Mantia
Personal Trainer

With a clientele ranging from a police academy to a telephone company to other fitness organizations and health clubs and individuals, Patti Mantia of the Mansfield, Massachusetts-based Fitness Firm has a lot of frequent flier miles. In addition to many European and Caribbean countries, she's been in most states, educating and certifying other trainers and instructors as well as providing personalized programs to individuals.

Mantia entered this field over fifteen years ago when she began teaching aerobics and people started asking her for individual attention. "Personal training used to be reserved for the very rich," she notes. "But now it's for anyone with a busy lifestyle or those who want to work toward a specific goal or event" such as a marathon. She keeps her client base small "because I'm on the road so much and want to be able to give everyone the time they need.

"Consumers are looking for education and certification," she continues, although she believes practical experience is necessary before attempting this field. "Trainers must keep abreast of the latest industry developments because clients are well-informed and count on your being up-to-date."

Traveling Nurse

Finally, a job for nurses who *don't* like routine, and prefer longer vacations than their colleagues who work for a single institution. Traveling nurses go from city to city, filling temporary vacancies at hospitals, nursing homes, and clinics, wherever someone's sick, pregnant, or resigns. Their employment agency generally finds them a furnished apartment and the position—after that, they are on their own. This job can definitely be an adventure, as anyone who's ever tried to navigate a strange city knows.

Most traveling nurses are registered nurses (RNs), with a minimum of one year's experience in their specialty. These specialties include pediatrics, oncology, emergency room medicine, intensive care, maternity, and others. You can become an RN in several ways: by getting an associate degree (ADN) diploma, after completing a two-year program offered at a community or junior college; by obtaining a bachelor of science (BSN) degree, after completing a four-to-five-year program at an accredited university; or through a two-to-three-year diploma program at a hospital. A BSN seems the most desirable path, leading to better jobs and graduate studies as well as higher pay.

Along with having a particular set of skills that enables them to quickly fit into the hospital team, traveling nurses must be flexible and willing to accept hospital policy. What is standard procedure in one place may be considered intrusive in another. Still, the nurse must have the confidence and experience to make day-to-day decisions without constantly consulting a supervisor.

Independence and a willingness to try new things and meet new people are other requirements. It can get lonely unless you have a specific interest or hobby. Church groups, computer bulletin boards, and adult education classes help assure continuity.

As in the nursing profession in general, jobs in this field are becoming more difficult to find. Although there was a shortage of nurses several years ago, the gap is being filled quickly by those attracted to the profession's stability. Still, hospitals appreciate the money they save in benefits and training by utilizing travelers, who also tend to be more reliable than local temporaries. Pay is comparable with other RN's, about $35,000 a year.

Another type of "traveling" involves working as a visiting or private duty nurse within one geographical area. Visiting RNs usually care for very ill patients and may be employed on a contract basis or by a local nursing agency. They are employed in homes, hospitals, rehabilitation facilities, and senior centers. Visiting nurses can also be licensed practical (LPN) or licensed vocational (LVN) nurses who have taken a year's study at a trade, technical, or vocational school. Although not as highly trained or paid as RNs, they provide basic bedside care to recovering patients, as well as prepare meals and teach family members simple nursing tasks. LPNs are especially useful in dealing with elderly patients who are not sick enough to go into a nursing home but need some specialized attention.

Associations

American Association of Colleges of Nursing
1 Dupont Circle, Suite 530
Washington, DC 20036
202/463-6930

American Nurses' Association
600 Maryland Ave. SW
Washington, DC 20024
202-554-4444

National Association for Practical Nurse Education and Service
1400 Spring Street, Suite 310
Silver Spring, MD 20910
301/588-2491

National Federation of Licensed Practical Nurses
P.O. Box 18088
Raleigh, NC 27619
919/781-4791

National League for Nursing
350 Hudson Street
New York, NY 10014
212/989-9393

Books

Caregiver, Caretaker. Summers, Caryn L. Mt. Shasta, CA: Commune-a-key, 1992.

The Hidden Dimension of Illness. Starck, Patricia and John P. McGovern, New York: National League for Nursing, 1992.
Independent Nursing Interventions. Snyder, Mariah, ed. New York: Wiley, 1985.
Nurses, Patients, and Families. Rosenthal, Carolyn J. New York: Springer, 1980.
Patient Teaching. Springhouse, PA: Springhouse, 1987
The Quality of Caring. Peters, Donna A., ed. Frederick, MD: Aspen, 1991.

Magazines

American Nurse
Concern
The Forum
Healthcare Nurse
Nightingale
Nurscene
Nurse Entrepreneur
Nursing
RN Magazine

Linda McKenney
Traveling Nurse

After two decades in a hospital setting, Linda McKenney, an emergency room nurse based in Ann Arbor, Michigan, decided to make a change. "I love nursing but hate hospital politics," she admits. The death of her father and grandfather were deciding factors: "I wanted to travel for a long time, but couldn't because they needed me."

Every three months or so, she loads up her Mazda with her personal items and heads to her next assignment. "My refrigerator magnets tell me that it's home," she half-jokes.

Over the past two years she's lived in or near Atlanta, Houston, Las Vegas, Oakland, and Long Island. "It's great, because you can go in and just do the job. I prefer to keep my work and private life separate, although it's fun getting to know new nurses and doctors. I have friends all over the country now."

> Food is an important part of a balanced diet.
>
> —FRAN LEBOWITZ

Food, Glorious Food

Caterer
Cooking Instructor
Food Consultant
Grocery Sample Demonstrator
Restaurant Meal Deliverer

Caterer

This may be the perfect job for those who think they can throw better parties than their friends. Caterers are the kitchen-hater's dream: they plan, shop, prepare, and clean up everything. And they get paid for doing what they enjoy.

Another bonus: This job requires little formal training, although many caterers take classes in hospitality management at local colleges, courses at cooking schools, or have equivalent experience. Their backgrounds can range from culinary institute graduates to restaurant service workers, to homemakers, to corporate escapees with a flair for the gourmet.

What successful caterers share in common, however, is an equal portion of cooking and business skills. Often the lack of the latter sabotages the former, so it's best to be as well-versed in taxes, zoning, insurance, local health regulations, cash and personnel management, and business planning as you are in perfecting a white chocolate mousse. Any mistake can be costly in terms of both economics and reputation. Not only will your customer likely refuse to pay the bill but everyone present will know it's your fault.

Before you meet with your first client, you must decide whether you're going to handle small affairs in people's homes or bigger events. You'll need to set fees and determine equipment requirements. Even the smallest caterer working out of his kitchen requires extra refrigeration, stove and oven space, utensils, and a large vehicle (such as a minivan) to transport the prepared food. Without these on hand, start-up can be quite expensive.

Setup times may vary from thirty minutes for a simple cocktail party in someone's living room to four or more hours for a big bash with multiple serving stations. And larger, more expensive events take months of planning, whereas several ten dollar-a-head dinners with fifty people might be equally or even more lucrative. Most caterers draw up a contract with each client to avoid misunderstandings.

Caterers arranging functions such as wedding receptions visit the site to determine the type of equipment needed. Along with renting tents if the event is outside, you'll be making sure there's enough food as well as tables, linens, and china, because running out would be tantamount to dusting your lemon chicken with chili powder instead of paprika.

Beginning caterers might want to go through a "dress rehearsal" before the actual event in case, say, they've forgotten to order salad forks or wine glasses for the six hundred guests. Such large quantities are not readily obtained on short notice. Here, obsessive list making and attention to detail definitely come in handy.

Determining your busiest seasons (often during spring and summer weddings and between Thanksgiving and New Year's) will help gauge how many employees you'll need to hire. Finding dependable helpers to serve and clean up is yet another challenge; college campuses and restaurants are often good sources.

Successful caterers find that they can control the volume of their business along with making pots of money (one Midwestern caterer claims it's "easy" to earn $100,000 a year), but they know where to shop and hardly ever say no to a good customer, even if it's at the last minute, on a holiday, or during the weekend. And their errors rarely eat into their revenue.

Associations

American Culinary Federation
P.O. Box 3466
St. Augustine, FL
904/824-4468

American Institute of Wine and Food
1550 Bryant Street, Suite 7000
San Francisco, CA 94103
415/255-3000

International Association of Culinary Professionals
304 W. Liberty Street, Suite 201
Louisville, KY 40202
502/581-9786

National Association of Catering Executives
304 W. Liberty Street
Louisville, KY 40202
502/583-3783

Books

Careers for Gourmets and Others Who Relish Food. Donovan, Mary. Lincolnwood, IL: NTC, 1993.

The Complete Caterer. Lawrence, Elizabeth. New York: Doubleday, 1992.
How to Open and Operate a Home-Based Catering Business. Vivaldo, Denise. Old Saybrook, CT: Globe-Pequot, 1993.
Kitchen Science. Hillman, Howard. New York: Macmillan, 1989.
Successful Catering. Splaver, Bernard. New York: Van Nostrand Reinhold, 1991.

Magazines

Cook
Fancy Foods
Food Arts
Food & Wine
Saveur
Gourmet
many others

Shawn Overstreet
Freelance Caterer

Although he works out of a successful deli, Shawn Overstreet of Columbus, Ohio, is captain of his own ship. He handles every aspect of a job, from preparing the contract to cleaning up. "Catering is very labor-intensive and hands-on, with not a lot of delegating," he observes.

Creativity is involved as well. "Cooking is instinctive and requires more than following a recipe. It's adding extra touches of flavor and making the food appealing through garnishes and presentation.

"People get nervous because they're throwing the occasion," he continues. "It's up to me to reassure them everything's under control." What takes the average person months to plan, Overstreet can pull together in a day. "My parents owned a restaurant, so I've done this all my life. It gets into your blood."

Cooking Instructor

Those who enjoy giving food preparation tips to friends and relatives might consider teaching cooking. You can start in your own home, providing private or small group lessons. Make sure you've cleared it with the local gendarmes, however. Nothing's more embarrassing than a visit by the health department after a nice feature on the six o'clock news. Before opening your doors for business, a quick call to area authorities will clear up misunderstandings regarding regulations and necessary permits.

Other entrées into this field include the local YM or YWCA, department stores, gourmet shops, and established cooking schools. As a teacher, you'll need to be a bit of a ham, along with knowing how to best prepare your specialty, ham or otherwise. You also need to be patient with the epicurically challenged, communicating clearly and demonstrating basic techniques. For some, cooking is an art; for others, a science; for still others, a near impossibility, so explanations should be understood by all.

This is not the place to leave out that special something that makes Grandma's brownies so scrumptious. Students will want to share their results with family and friends, and they'll credit you either way. They're paying money to learn from your talent; if you want to keep the brownies a secret, serve them at home. You may also find yourself cleaning up messes; students come to have fun and create, not to scrub pots.

Curriculum is another important ingredient. Students should know exactly what they'll be learning as well as the required equipment or premade food to bring to the classroom. There are almost as many different classes as recipes: French, pastry, vegetarian, Kosher, bread baking, sauces, etc., as well as the basic methods of preparation and planning. Successful instructors may find their vocation leads to the establishment of their own cooking school, publication of cookbooks, TV shows, and even possibly fame à la James Beard or Julia Child.

Salaries are delectable for something so seemingly easy to whip up. Instructors with established schools can make up to

$60,000 a year; even smaller places pay around $30,000 or so. Independent operators can do as well or better, as long as they "fold in" the cost of ingredients, overhead, and advertising. Although they may teach evenings and weekends, instructors' hours are shorter and more reasonable than those of the average chef or food service worker.

Along with a background in food handling and preparation (through taking courses yourself or work experience), it's best to be up on the latest industry techniques. Through your students, you'll have the satisfaction of knowing your concoctions will live longer than the next digestive cycle.

Associations

James Beard Foundation
167 West 12th Street
New York, NY 10011
212/675-4984

Culinary Institute of America
433 Albany Post Road
Hyde Park, NY 12538
800/285-4627

New York Restaurant School
27 West 34th Street
New York, NY 10001
212/226-5500

See also Caterer

Books

Food Work. Sims-Bell, Barbara. Santa Barbara: Advocacy Press, 1993.

How to Turn a Passion for Food Into Profit. Kleeman, Elayne and Jeanne Voltz. New York: Rawson Wade, 1979.

Opportunities in Culinary Careers. Donovan, Mary. Lincolnwood, IL: NTC, 1990.

Teaching and You. Evans, Jack and Martha Brueckner. Boston: Allyn and Bacon, 1992.

The Teaching Marketplace. Brodsky, Bart and Janet Geis. Berkeley: Community Resource Institute, 1992

Magazines

ArtCulinare
Best Recipes
Cookbook Digest
Culinary Review
Fine Cooking
Food & Wine
Guide to Cooking Schools

Chef Wayne Almquist, Instructor, Culinary Institute of America

Wayne Almquist's résumé reads like a Who's Who of restaurants: He apprenticed at the Waldorf-Astoria Hotel, was a chef at the Four Seasons Restaurant and the Paul Revere Room in New York City, was an executive chef at an exclusive Long Island country club and owned eateries in the New York-New Jersey area.

For more than twenty years, however, he has taught at the Culinary Institute of America in Hyde Park, New York. "You need a passion for both cooking and teaching," he observes. "It came naturally to me because, as a chef, I was always showing people how to do things." But he's noticed a big change in the past few years: "Now people are more willing to share information. Before they were afraid someone would steal their job."

Almquist enjoys the give and take of the institute, although even he had to "audition" by providing a demo and cooking lunch for those who hired him. "It's a lot easier to take a chef and train him or her to be an instructor than vice versa."

Food Consultant

This job may raise a few eyebrows, especially in less populated areas. Are there really "food consultants" or is it just a nice term for unemployment?

Anyone who lives in a city knows restaurants open and close with astonishing regularity, while certain food trends emerge—for example, Southwestern cooking and California spa cuisine. Food consultants are often the people responsible for these eateries hitting at the right moment to attract influential clientele. Their wide range of knowledge—dining area and kitchen design; menu setup and formulation; how to train employees and managers; even the proper shape and selection of silverware, glasses, and china—help make the restaurant unique. Even if investors utilize other experts to put the various components together, they will likely need a consultant to make the whole concept come together.

Food consultants can be from different backgrounds—architecture, design, nutrition, food service, culinary, or most preferably, a combination of all of these. Many study an academic discipline for years, then further their educations by working in a restaurant or going to chef's school. Trimming carrots properly is as important as being up on the latest fads.

Consultants wear many hats—designing cooking equipment, giving menus a facelift, reformulating recipes for a large company, even producing publicity and training videos for new products. They must be well-versed on whatever projects they take on, and may find themselves continually doing research or attending additional courses.

Finding jobs however, may be as tricky as the work itself. Eateries have a high mortality rate and are expensive to set up and maintain. Many people dream about owning a restaurant but lack funds to back up their big plans. So you'll need to screen potential clients carefully, perhaps asking them to pay you weekly rather than at the end of a job. It's nearly impossible to squeeze money out of a Chapter 11 enterprise.

This field's also a lot like writing screenplays; for every five that are optioned, only one of your concepts may see fruition. So you might find yourself taking odd or short-term jobs to help meet bills, acting as an assistant chef or night manager until the next "dream assignment" comes along.

But there's nothing like getting paid up to $100,000 a year for your creations (although consultants starting out earn much less). And investors are putting their money on you so you had better deliver a product in excellent taste.

Associations

American Hotel and Motel Education Institute
1213 Bakers Way
Manhattan, KS 66502
913/537-4750

Council on Hotel, Restaurant and Institutional Education
1200 17th Street, NW
Washington, DC 20036
202/331-5990

Foodservice Consultants Society International
304 W. Liberty Street, Suite 201
Louisville, KY 40202
502/583-3783

Institute of Food Technologists
221 N. LaSalle Street
Chicago, IL 60601
312/782-8284

National Restaurant Association
350 S. Wacker Drive, Suite 1400
Chicago, IL 60606
800/765-2122

Books

Careers for Gourmets and Others Who Relish Food. Donovan, Mary. Lincolnwood, IL: NTC, 1993.
Design and Layout of Foodservice Facilities. Birchfield, John. New York: Van Nostrand Reinhold, 1988.
Food Service Marketing. Anderson, Linda K. Austin, TX: Center for Occupational Curriculum Development, 1982.

Magazines

Food Management
Nation's Restaurant News
Restaurant Business
Restaurants and Institutions
Restaurant Trends

Francine Jarvis
Food Consultant

Her background in architecture and professional training as a chef helped consultant Francine Jarvis get several Manhattan restaurants started. She has also worked in all aspects of the restaurant business, from managing to clean-up. "In this business, you can make good money, but you really need to know what you're doing," she says.

Jarvis looks to sophisticated urban centers for work. There "you'll find an appreciation of new or novel dining experiences not obvious in less populated areas." She has also had her disappointments, such as creating several low-fat recipes for a major fast-food chain that were never utilized. "It was decided that people like the taste of 'real' burgers and fries."

Jarvis's travels have taken her to both coasts and abroad; currently she's setting up a takeout shop in Hong Kong. "This is a wonderful field for women. If you're willing to work hard and learn, your knowledge will get you jobs, no matter who you are."

Grocery Sample Demonstrator

You see them at the grocery store or anywhere else food is sold in quantity—the cheerful ladies (and a few men) who cook and distribute appetizing morsels, urging you to try the product. Those who wish to become a member of this coupon-bearing corps need a sturdy pair of feet, a willingness to take rejection, and an enjoyment of food preparation and serving. It's a lot easier than being a waiter or waitress and usually pays better, too (before tips, that is).

However, this is not the job to set the culinary world on fire. As an independent contractor or employee of a demonstration company, you'll be expected to be dependable, prompt, and sometimes bring your own equipment. The enterprise that hires you will be counting on you to increase sales of their product, so you need to know the company line. Sales experience, in addition to a high school education or equivalent, is extremely helpful; your employer usually takes care of training specifics regarding the item, its preparation, and safety rules. Before you get your own star turn, you'll likely do a shift or two with an established demonstrator.

This can be the ideal part-time or second job. Most demonstrators work shifts of about seven hours that include setup and breakdown times. Since stores are busiest in the evenings and on weekends, that's when your services will be most in demand. Thanksgiving and Christmas are also hectic, providing an often needed holiday income boost. Pay is in the $7 per hour range in larger cities; less if the area's not as populated.

Some products are more appealing than others, so that's where you'll need some imagination. Eye-catching displays, creative recipes, and knowledge of nutritional value help boost sales. If you're asked to work with the same product for several weeks or days in a row, you can prepare it differently each time, so customers will look forward to seeing what you've done next.

Food can be arranged in an appetizing and attractive manner; for instance, samples of rippled cheese can be put on different kinds of bread with a frilly toothpick instead of being placed on an unadorned plate with plain slices. Potential customers may need a little gentle persuasion to try something new, but don't push chocolate cake on someone who claims to be diabetic.

Start-up costs can be minimal—you can use utensils, electric frying pans, toaster ovens, even a portable microwave from home, if that's what the job calls for. And if business is slow, you can always sneak a bite of the samples.

Associations

Food Marketing Institute
800 Connecticut Ave., NW, Suite 500
Washington, DC 20006
202/452-8444

Grocery Manufacturers of America
1010 Wisconsin Ave., NW, Suite 900
Washington, DC 20007
202/337-9400

National Food Brokers Association
2100 Reston Parkway, Suite 400
Reston, VA 22091
703/758-7790

Books

Competitive Strategy Analysis in the Food System. Cotterill, Ronald. Boulder: Westview, 1993.

Food Merchandising. German, Gene and Theodore Leed. New York: Lebhar-Friedman, 1992.

The Food Retailing Industry. Marion, Bruce, et al. New York: Praeger, 1979.

Modern Supermarket Operations. Gold, Faye, et al. New York: Fairchild, 1981.

Supermarket Merchandising and Management. Peak, Hugh S. and Ellen. Englewood Cliffs, NJ: Prentice-Hall, 1977.

Magazines

Food Herald
Food Merchandise Advocate
Food People
Grocery Marketing
Issues Bulletin
New Product News

Dee Vanyo
Demonstrator

Dee Vanyo started as a grocery demonstrator twenty years ago "because I got paid to do what I enjoy the most—be around people and act like a hostess." Today she owns a business that hires demonstrators for stores in the Cleveland, Ohio area.

"This field has grown a lot," she observes. "Research has shown that handing someone a coupon is far more effective than getting the coupon from a point of purchase machine or a mailer. Today's health-conscious customers also expect you to know all about the product—sodium and fat content, how it will affect their cholesterol. You need to be an expert on what you're selling."

Vanyo recommends finding a demonstration company and staying with it, even if you're an independent contractor. "They're looking for professionals who are available when they need them. If you're off on another job, they'll call someone else."

Restaurant Meal Deliverer

This seems like the perfect opportunity for the nineties. Not only are people staying at home more and "cocooning," but they have no time to mess with preparing elaborate meals (is there a contradiction here?). Regardless, restaurant meal delivery has arrived and you can be at the forefront, either as a deliverer or as the owner of a franchise or your own business.

If you choose to be a deliverer, you'll be given food in special containers that will keep it hot or cold as needed. Your mission is to find the address as quickly as possible and get the meal there at the expected time. For this, you'll get paid $8 to $12 an hour, which includes hourly rate, tips, and commission. But you'll need to avoid sharp turns and sudden stops or the customers will notice when their green beans end up in their veal scallopini. A good driving record and presentable appearance are a must, so keep tattoos and nipple rings under cover.

Those who own a delivery service face a few more challenges. You'll need to convince restaurants that you're reliable and that they'll increase their business by signing up with your service. Then the public should get wind of what's cooking; this is best done through door-to-door canvassing in yuppified apartment complexes, condos, and residential areas. Flyers should illustrate the wide variety of choices and provide sample listings from various menus. Obviously, the more restaurants that participate, the wider the appeal.

You can also emphasize that in addition to getting their favorite entrées in the privacy of their own homes, customers will actually be saving money on beverages and hefty tips. Of course, there's a delivery fee (about three dollars, depending upon the city's size). But it's still cheaper for a family of four to eat at home using your service. *And* that's *after* tipping the driver his or her 10 percent.

However, start-up costs can run into several thousand dollars. These include a franchise fee (if applicable), rent of a space and overhead, such as electricity and phone costs, computers for record keeping, food delivery bags, two-way radios for communication with the drivers, uniforms, and insurance. Customers rarely see the inside of your operation so a basic table and chairs are all you'll need.

A background in business and sales is also important, as is knowledge of the restaurant industry. A franchise can be very helpful here; they have set up this type of business before and can provide guidance. But check it out first and make sure it's legitimate. Any new and fairly untried field can be full of fly-by-nights.

Your salary will depend upon how much business you can obtain at both the restaurant and customer ends. But by delivering the goods, you can really turn up your volume.

Associations

National Restaurant Association
350 S. Wacker Drive, Suite 1400
Chicago, IL 60606
800/765-2122

Books

Meal Delivery Manual. Hetherington, Peter. Laguna Nigel, CA: Mail Delivery Ltd., updated regularly. Available only from author: 24275 LaHermosa Ave., Laguna Nigel, CA 92677.

Food Delivery Service. Irvine, CA: Entrepreneur Group, 1990.

Magazines

Food Management
Meal Delivery Digest
Nation's Restaurant News
Restaurant Business
Restaurants and Institutions
Restaurant Trends

Brant Druhot
Delivery Service Owner

As a sales rep who exported commodities to developing Third World countries, Brad Druhot made a major career change when he purchased the local franchise for Takeout Taxi. This Richmond, Virginia, enterprise covers the entire area of over 850,000 people and, for Druhot, has translated into mucho dinero and dinners.

One must be able to deal with the public, however, and that means being a good communicator. "Along with listening to the customers, you need to create appealing advertising, such as a menu booklet describing what you have to offer. This involves marketing, sales, and managerial skills.

"Being an owner is a lot more work than being an employee, but I like being resposible for my own success."

However much you knock on nature's door, she will never answer you in comprehensible words.

—IVAN TURGENEV

The Great Outdoors

Arborist
Cowboy
Landscaper
Ornithologist
Park Ranger
Raft Guide
Shepherd
Smoke Jumper

Arborist

I think that I shall never see
A poem lovely as a tree.

When Joyce Kilmer penned those immortal words at the turn of the century, no one knew how complicated caring for our leafy friends would become. Today's arborists (their specialty is called arboriculture) select and transplant trees; prune, repair, fertilize, and brace them; manage pests (human, plant disease, and insect); and make sure trees grow properly. They also protect trees on construction sites, appraise damaged or destroyed trees, and provide expert evaluations on all aspects of tree care. They can cultivate a lot of green stuff—up to $100,000 a year for full-fledged sales-management representatives.

Along with studying arboriculture, forestry, horticulture, plant science, pest management, and natural resources, most successful arborists have a degree from an accredited state college, technical or vocational school as well as extensive field experience. A master's degree or Ph.D. in a related specialty, such as etymology (the study of insects) is not uncommon. Because changes are many and developments rapid, even accredited arborists continue their education through home study and agency-sponsored courses, opting for voluntary certification through the International Society of Arboriculture.

In this occupation, you truly start at the top. Field work involves climbing trees and using saws; working with fertilizers, pesticides, and other dangerous chemicals; and utilizing safety procedures and equipment. A good sense of balance and upper body strength, along with a willingness to be out in all kinds of weather are a must. Those with a fear of heights need not apply. Along with diagnosing and curing tree ailments, arborists must also deal with owners, who may have definite, and often misguided, ideas of how a situation should be handled.

Arboriculture has several branches of specialization. The commercial end, where many jobs can be found, involves working for a private individual or concern. Those in sales (sometimes called estimators) visit the property and decide what needs to be done, be it pruning, insect control, removal, or fertilization. Salaries for those just out of college begin at around $25,000, with remuneration growing along with experience. Pay for the street crew—those who actually implement the estimator's recommendations—can be in the $25,000 to $35,000 range, but doesn't climb much higher, despite the increase in hazards. So there's greater turnover in the latter job.

Municipal arboriculture/urban forestry is similar to commercial work, except arborists also deal with trees and plants on streets, in parks, and on the grounds of public buildings. Along with helping preserve trees on construction sites, they develop and enforce various laws pertaining to trees, keep detailed records, and manage forest stands in watersheds or public parks.

Utility arboriculture relates to the maintenance of trees close to power lines, a potentially electrifying career path. Other aspects encompass prevention of power outages, management of trees so they don't interfere with right-of-way travel on railroads or highways, testing new line clearance and vegetation control methods, and review of wildlife management programs. These arborists also educate the public regarding proper tree maintenance near utility lines and suitable species for planting in these areas (presumably slow-growing).

Arboriculture is but an offshoot of a number of careers related to trees including forestry, forestry technology, range conservation, soil conservation, and others. Kilmer would have been proud.

Associations

American Society of Consulting Arborists
5130 W. 101st Circle
Westminster, CO 80030
303/466-2722

International Society of Arboriculture
P.O. Box GG
Savoy, IL 61874-9902
217/355-9411

National Arborist Association
The Meeting Place Mall, P.O. Box 1094
Route 101
Amherst, NH 03031-1094
800/733-2622

Books

The Care and Feeding of Trees. Murphy, Richard C. New York: Crown, 1983.

The Essential Pruning Companion. Maline, John. North Pomfret, VT: Trafalgar Square, 1992.

An Introduction to Pruning. Johns, Patrick. New York: Gallery, 1991.

A New Tree Biology. Shigo, Alex L. Durham, NH: Shigo & Trees, 1989.

Pruning: A Practical Guide. McHoy, Peter. New York: Abbeville, 1993.

Tree Maintenance. Pirone, P.P. New York: Oxford University, 1988.

Magazines

Arbor Age
Arboricultural Consultant
Arborist News
Journal of Arboriculture

Larry Hall
Arborist

An arborist since 1948, Larry Hall of Wheeling, Illinois has seen a lot of growth, and not just in the trees he's tended. "Mechanization changed everything," he observes. "For instance, we didn't have chain saws, but pruned by hand. In the past, we used ropes and ladders; now there are aerial towers to get to trees. Rather than picking up each branch and loading it onto a truck, brush chippers condense it into bite-sized chunks of wood, which are used for mulching. It's much safer and more efficient."

But the biggest change has been in education. "Most key people have a bachelor's degree in urban forestry. In the past, training didn't seem to make much difference, as long as you loved trees, and were hale, hearty, and vigorous."

The spread of Dutch Elm disease in the fifties and sixties, he believes, had much to do with raising the public consciousness about trees. "We lost a great number of street trees. People realized we'd better take care of them." And the jobs keep on sprouting.

Cowboy

They are the stuff from which movie and literary legends are made, but are there any real cowboys left? The answer is: Yes, no, and maybe.

In the few remaining states where wilderness remains—although even that is rapidly dwindling—there is still a call for folks with roping, calving, and herding experience as well as the dozens of other miscellaneous tasks that come with being a cowboy. Most of these "cowboys" are ranchers, however, whereas in the past, there was a major distinction between the two. Cowboys were free agents who never owned property or socialized with their bosses and lived five to six in a bunkhouse. They were also mostly single.

Economics has forced most ranchers to let their hired hands go. When they do need someone, it's often temporary and for about $700 to $1200 a month (room, board, and horse feed included). Tenderfoots need not apply.

More often than not, ranchers and their families do most of the cowboy chores and earn a fairly decent living as long as the weather and market conditions cooperate. The work is cyclical; each year they "round up" cattle on horseback to take to market or fresher grazing grounds. They utilize pickups, cook by the campfire, and sleep under the stars when they're on the trail. Some of the rougher aspects of cowboying include branding and administering medical treatment to cattle and shooting dinner. It's not an easy or lucrative life, but it's uncomplicated and honest.

Those who wish to be more than urban cowboys but don't want to get too grubby can find employment on the rodeo circuit or on dude ranches. They can learn the basics (saddle and bareback bronco riding, bull riding, calf roping, steer wrestling) at one of several rodeo schools. Along with safety skills and proper riding habits, students are taught the fundamentals on gentle animals and bucking machines before attempting "rank stock." You'll find out right quick whether you've got the grit for cowboying (both a verb and a noun in most Western states).

Those without the endurance for the tough and not-always-profitable rodeo circuit might find employment at a dude ranch. The best opportunities can be on working ranches, where guests pay to participate in roundups, brandings, and cattle drives. Salaries vary according to the ranch and level of experience.

Romantics often overlook the fact that cowboying can be pricey. Hats, spurs, chaps, boots, jackets, and belts can set you back a couple thousand dollars. And that won't even include the expense and upkeep of your horse.

Associations

American National Cattle Women
5240 S. Quebec
Englewood, CO 80155
303/694-0313

Dude Ranchers Association
Box 471
Laporte, CO 80535
303/223-8440

International Professional Rodeo Association
2304 Exchange Ave.
Oklahoma City, OK 73108
405/235-6540

National Cattleman's Association
P.O. Box 3469
Englewood, CO 80155
303/694-0305

Professional Rodeo Cattleman's Association
101 Prorodeo Drive
Colorado Springs, CO 80919
719/593-8840

Books

Be Tough or Be Gone. Davis, Tom. Alamosa, CO: Northern Trails, 1984.
The Cowboy Life. Morris, Michele. New York: Fireside, 1993.
The Modern Cowboy. Erickson, John. Lincoln: University of Nebraska, 1981.
The Working Cowboy's Manual. Ward, Fay E. New York: Bonanza, 1983.

Magazines

Cowboy Magazine
Dude Rancher
Ketch Pin
Rodeo News
Rope Burns
Trail Rider
many others

Fred Paulek
Cowboy

Fred Paulek of Hesperus, Colorado, rides the range like his father and grandfather, but sees his way of life rapidly coming to an end. He lives on the same thousand-acre ranch that his grandfather homesteaded, but his children have chosen other occupations.

Although Paulek herds his cattle in the time-honored way, he has a great respect for modern technology. "Horses and cattle need a lot of doctoring, and there's always a new or experimental product on the market. You have to be dedicated and treat it like a business." He is also gun shy about liability insurance and heads that off at the pass by doing most of the work himself.

Along with a fondness for poetry, beer, and pickups (both female and vehicular), cowboys need to have a wide variety of skills "from bookkeeping to management to fixing fences to irrigating. You've got to be able to handle whatever it takes to get the job done."

Landscaper

Most states require licensing for individuals who design the land surrounding residential areas, public and industrial parks, college campuses, shopping centers, golf courses, and others. So just hanging out a shingle and picking up graph paper, shovels, rakes, and other equipment won't take root. Graduates of landscape architecture programs take an internship in a large firm, gaining the experience needed to be licensed by the Landscape Architectural Accreditation Board.

Minimum requirements include a specialized bachelor's degree, or a three-year master's degree for undergraduates majoring in another field. The curriculum includes surveying, design and construction, ecology, and city and regional planning as well as plant and soil sciences, geology, design and color theory, and general management. Students are assigned actual projects, often working with new technologies such as computer-assisted design, geographic information systems, and video simulation.

Licensed landscape architects spend much time at the site. They analyze the climate, soil, slope of land, drainage, and vegetation, in addition to determining exteriors. Along with examining the area from different angles, they note where the sunlight falls during the day and evaluate the effect on the surrounding territory. They determine what exteriors help preserve the environment and plan the location of buildings, roads, and walkways. With budgetary and legal requirements in mind, they then work up drawings and written estimates, culminating in a scale model of the design. After that, they incorporate any changes and help supervise construction.

Besides having a strong creative flair, landscapers must be able to solve problems, deal with other professionals, be proficient in design, and have good writing and communications skills. They can work for the government, for corporations, for engineering or architectural firms, or for themselves. Project locations can range from hazardous waste sites to waterfront developments to zoos to private homes. However, most of the money is in commercial rather than residential assignments.

Salaries rise in proportion to skill; landscapers with only bachelor's degrees start at about $20,000 a year, while those with a master's earn approximately $10,000 more. Well-established landscape architects may find themselves pulling in six-figure incomes.

Although the economy isn't always conducive to new construction, an increasing need to preserve what we've got and create environmentally sound new developments make this job a keeper. Not many people can look like they're meandering around and collect a paycheck at the same time.

Associations

American Society of Landscape Architects
4401 Connecticut Ave., NW, Fifth floor
Washington, DC 20008
800/727-2655

Council of Landscape Architecture Registration Boards
12700 Fair Lakes Circle, Suite 110
Fairfax, VA 22033
703/818-1300

Books

Basic Elements of Landscape Architectural Design. Booth, Norman K. Prospect Heights, IL: Waveland, 1990.
Designing the New Landscape. Lyall, Sutherland. New York: Van Nostrand Reinhold, 1991.
Introduction to Landscape Design. Motloch, John L. New York: Van Nostrand Reinhold, 1991.
Landscape Design. Hannebaum, Leroy. Englewood Cliffs, NJ: Prentice-Hall, 1994.
Landscape Graphics. Reid, Grant. New York: Whitney Library of Design, 1987.

Magazines

Landscape Architecture
Landscape Architectural Forum
Landscape and Irrigation
Landscape Design
many others

Andrew Smith
Landscape Architect

Although he's a recent graduate, Andrew Smith of Johns Island, South Carolina, isn't afraid to get his hands dirty. The firm he works for specializes in upscale residential design, and he is already involved in several projects.

"It's like being a painter," he observes. "The site is an empty canvas and you figure out how the landscape best complements the house." If it's a new build, he helps determine the optimal location for the home, then starts working on the "hardscape"—the design of sidewalks, driveways, terraces, decks, and so forth. Smith then decides which plants go where. "Depending on the size of the job, the process can take from a few months to up to three or four years.

"You want to evoke certain moods and feelings, making sure the end product is comfortable, safe, and pleasing." However, Smith cautions against those who think they can become landscapers by working in, say, a garden center. "Along with scientific characteristics of the environment, you need to understand the basic principles of design."

Ornithologist

Ornithology is birdwatching taken to its highest power. The scientific study of birds encompasses their biology, ecology, behavior, anatomy, physiology, and evolution as well as veterinary science, wildlife management, and conservation. Still, most experts began as kids gawking at ravens, robins, and bluejays with a pair of binoculars. Unfortunately, jobs in this field can be as rare as hens' teeth, so you need to be trained in other kinds of work as well.

Where you go to college and what program you study is important—some courses emphasize theory while others are practical, some focus on cellular and molecular biology while others stress field biology. You will also take classes in general biology, botany, zoology, mathematics, statistics, biochemistry, computers, physical sciences, and foreign languages. And it's wise to have a backup degree in a related field such as toxicology, wildlife management, paleontology, physiology, or endocrinology.

Research assistanceships and publishing in scientific journals while you're in school help, as do working or volunteering at a university, park, wildlife refuge, nature conservancy, bird sanctuary, zoo, or museum. These are places where jobs can be found after you complete your masters' or Ph.D. The federal government, one of the few employers that hires ornithologists with a bachelor's degree, offers positions at the United States Fish and Wildlife Service, the National Park Service, the Forest Service, the Bureau of Land Management, and more.

Many ornithologists divide their time between teaching, research, and administration. You can be a curator at a museum and teach at a university, or be a college professor who does research. Ornithologists can also find positions as keepers and curators in zoos, as wildlife managers at state fish and game agencies, and as analysts of public conservation policies or supervisors of sanctuary systems for Audubon societies, bird observatories, and related organizations.

Although they don't work for a song, salaries range from $20,000 to $55,000 a year in the public and most academic sectors. Those hired by corporations and privately funded universities may earn considerably more, and consultation is always a possibility for extra income.

But most ornithologists aren't in it for the money; not only do they get to pursue what fascinates them, they can fly off to the far corners of the Earth seeking knowledge and various species. Their avian friends truly understand how much that freedom means.

Associations

American Ornithologists' Union
Department of Ornithology
Museum of Natural History
Washington, DC 20560
202/357-2051

American Birding Association
P.O. Box 6599
Colorado Springs, CO 80934
719/578-9703

National Audubon Society
950 Third Ave.
New York, NY 10022
212/832-3200

Books

A Guide to Bird Behavior. Stokes, Donald and Lillian. Boston: Little, Brown, 1969.
An Introduction to Ornithology. Wallace, George John and Harold D. Mahan. New York: Macmillan, 1975.
Watching Birds. Pasquier, Roger F. Boston: Houghton Mifflin, 1977.
The World of Birds. Corral, Michael. Chester, CT: Globe Pequot, 1989.

Magazines

The Auk
Bird Conservation International
The Condor
Journal of Field Ornithology
North American Bird Bander
Living Bird
Western Bird
many others

Dr. Ned Johnson
Ornithology Professor and Researcher

Along with being a professor at the department of integrative biology at the University of California in Berkeley, Dr. Ned Johnson is the curator of a large research museum there. The collection consists of about 180,000 birds, all of which are dead. "We loan the skins, skeletons, and tissues to different researchers," he explains. "They utilize the information to work on, for example, medicine and cures for illnesses, both bird and human." The museum also has recordings of bird songs.

Johnson's own work focuses on how new types of avians evolve. "I study color, size, genetics, and how they relate to different zones of the environment. We can determine genetic variations as well as biological diversity."

One of his favorite parts of the job is the travel. In examining species, he says, "you get to see the world and do a lot of camping out." He acknowledges that it can be dangerous: "Sometimes the people aren't friendly and there's always the possibility of poisonous insects and disease."

Park Ranger

If you like uniforms, this may be the job for you. You might also get a Park Ranger Field Kit, which has, among other things, field glasses, compass, handcuffs, measuring tape, tools, a flashlight, special rations in case you're caught without food, and that nifty-looking, wide-brimmed hat. The problem is, you have to go through a lot of training and tests to get there.

The 360-site National Park Service (NPS) has over thirteen thousand full-time employees, of which less than half are uniformed rangers. But competition can be keen, with thousands of people applying for even temporary summer positions. In order to work in either law enforcement or as a naturalist-historian, you need a minimum of two years of college and to be on the Office of Personnel Management register. The latter requires taking and passing an examination for entry-level government positions.

College background can range from the earth sciences to archeology, to park and recreation management, to law enforcement, to business or public administration, to sociology. Here is one field where a liberal arts education comes in handy. It also helps to have worked part-time or as a volunteer at a park.

Park rangers specializing in law enforcement patrol the area to protect property and prevent unlawful hunting; inspect trees for disease and contain renegade animals; enforce regulations; investigate complaints, disturbances, and trespassers; and perform search and rescue operations. Some are lone rangers working alone as fire spotters; general duties also encompass forest or structural fire control. Entry-level forest police perform less menacing tasks like operating campgrounds, replenishing firewood, and administering safety inspections.

Naturalist and historian rangers gather historical, topographical, and scientific data about an area, developing and interpreting it for various programs. They also demonstrate folk arts and crafts, emphasizing the cultural features of the park. Venues can range from forests to lake shores to battlefields to archeological properties to seashores. Each ranger is responsible for his or her own presentation; beginners provide information to visitors and lead guided tours.

As with most government jobs, you must have a certain number of years of experience to be promoted. Most entry level positions are at the GS-5 or GS-7 level, paying from about \$19,000 to \$23,000 per annum as of this writing. More experienced rangers make around \$30,000, with supervisors and lifers capping the salary range at \$45,000 to \$50,000. The government also offers excellent health and retirement benefits. In addition, rangers have the option of employment anywhere in the country; assignments vary from the Washington Monument to the Statue of Liberty to the badlands of South Dakota to Mount Ranier in Washington State and hundreds of points between. Transfers in this job are never boring.

Those wanting to work as local-level park rangers should apply to their state, city, or county government. They still get the glamour of the uniform, and may not have to take a test.

Associations

Federal Job Information Center
Check local listings under "Federal government" and state/local parks in your telephone book.

National Parks and Conservation Association
1776 Massachusetts Ave., NW, Suite 200
Washington, DC 20036
202/223-6722

U.S. Department of the Interior
National Park Service
P.O. Box 37127
Washington, DC 20013-7127
202/208-4621
Information line: 202/208-4747

U.S. Office of Personnel Management
1900 E Street, NW
Washington, DC 20415
202/606-1700

Books

Desert Solitaire: A Season in the Wilderness. Abbey, Edward. New York: Simon and Schuster, 1990.

Park Ranger. Colby, C. B. New York: Coward, McCann and Geoghegan, 1971.

Magazines

Helping Out in the Outdoors
National Parks Magazine
Parks and Grounds Management
Parks
Parks and Recreation

Tom Tankersley
Interpretive Ranger

"There's no given path to becoming a park ranger," says Tom Tankersley, who works in Yellowstone National Park in Wyoming. "The most important strategy is getting experience so you can compete for the position."

Employed by the NPS for over twenty years, Tankersley worked at Richmond National Battlefield Park, Independence National Historical Park, George Washington's birthplace, and others before coming to Yellowstone. As assistant chief of interpretive operations, he supervises naturalist rangers who operate the visitor centers, organize educational hikes, and perform evening campfire programs.

"You need to be a social person with good communications skills," he says. "Your program must be original and not a canned presentation developed by someone else."

Tankersley says that with three million visitors a year, "we see quite a cross section of personalities and behavior. Occasionally people are disgruntled but most are on vacation and in search of information and new experiences."

Raft Guide

As a raft guide you can journey down the most beautiful rivers in the world and get paid for it. You can enjoy meals and sleep amidst untouched scenery and wildlife while experiencing the continual excitement and challenge of the rapids. And whitewater rafting and kayaking have become an increasingly popular form of recreation, with commercial rafting schools and companies proliferating. Is this a dream come true, or what?

Well, yes, if you're the right person for the job. But be aware that you will have to do without many of the comforts of civilization and will have to depend on your own resources. Rafting can be cold, wet, and lonely; there's not much money to be made; and the natives (your clients and other people you encounter on the river) can be unfriendly.

As a raft guide, you'll need to be physically fit to load and unpin rafts, handle launchings, and throw and maneuver ropes. Guides should also be certified as emergency medical technicians, which involves taking a 120-hour course Red Cross course in first aid and rescue. You must also be trained in boat navigation, maintenance, and repair as well as in camping and outdoor cooking techniques.

Total familiarity with the route is essential, whether it be for a few hours or several days, Rapids are evaluated according to their difficulty, with Class I being the most placid and Classes V and VI being dangerous. Most tours are for Class IV and below, but even these can be hazardous. You need to know every current, eddy, bend, ledge and other topographical nuance in advance.

Guides must be on the lookout for "holes," depressions behind rocks where the water forms a fast-moving vortex often strong enough to flip the raft. They must be prepared to deal with sudden rainstorms, which affect the run of the river. When someone falls in the water, guides need to watch for subtle symptoms of hypothermia, a life-threatening condition that occurs when body temperature drops drastically.

Finding a job can be almost as unpredictable as the rapids themselves. Persistence is the key here. Hanging around rafting outposts and gaining river experience is more likely to produce assignments than mailing out résumés and making phone calls.

You can train at commercial whitewater schools, specialized outdoor equipment shops, and whitewater clubs. Even some colleges and universities offer courses. Check out their credentials however, before investing your money. You can also learn on your own or under the guidance of a professional. Most beginners start with Class I rapids and work their way up.

Pay varies, with experienced guides earning $80 to $100 a day, and juniors making between $50 and $60. The season can be short, so guides wander gypsy-like to other rivers or take part-time employment in construction or at ski lodges. It's a great life for those who like to keep it simple.

Associations

America Outdoors
P.O. Box 1348
Knoxville, TN 37901
615/524-4814

American Whitewater Affiliation
P.O. Box 85
Phoenicia, NY 12464
914/688-5569

National Organization for River Sports
212 W. Cheyenne Mountain Blvd
Colorado Springs, CO 80906
719/579-8754

Books

The Basic Essentials of Rafting. Ellison, Jib. Merrillville, IN: ICS, 1991.

Path of the Paddle. Mason, Bill. Toronto: Van Nostrand Reinhold, 1980.

The White-Water Raft Book. Watters, Ron. Seattle: Pacific Search Press, 1984.

Whitewater Rafting. McGinnis, William. New York: Times Books, 1975.

Wild Rivers of North America. Jenkinson, Michael. New York: Dutton, 1973.

Magazines

Adventure Magazine
Adventure Weekend
American Rivers
American Whitewater Journal
Canoe
Currents

Bill Blackstock
Raft Guide and Teacher

"The first thing raft guides have to do is take a vow of poverty," half-jokes Bill Blackstock of El Prado, New Mexico. "Most of us live frugally so we can take a few off months each year and travel."

Along with having a cool head in emergencies, guides must also be good storytellers. "You need to know the geology, biology, and natural and cultural history of the area. You're with the customers constantly, so you want to keep them entertained. Find whatever local aspect interests you and take it from there.

"You never know what people are like until you put them in a wilderness situation," he continues. "Regardless of whether they're nice or mean, they need to know you're not there to wait on them and that on the river, you're in charge. Doing this tactfully is the most difficult part of the job" and can mean the difference between a safe and enjoyable trip and jeopardizing everyone.

A guide-teacher since 1976, Blackstock could be considered an "ancient mariner" of whitewater rafting. "For me, this is the best life. I'd rather handle a swift water emergency than sit in rush hour traffic."

Shepherd

Shepherding today is far more than ushering cute lambs from point A to point B with a trusty staff and loyal collie. The multimillion dollar sheep industry relies heavily on technology, agribusiness, and the latest in medical developments. So in order to make a living at it, a degree in agriculture and animal science or farm experience is recommended.

Along with knowledge of the various breeds of sheep (Dorset, Suffolk, Shropshire, Romney, et al.) and their characteristics, you'll need to understand reproductive cycles, overall health, general nutrition, and genetics as well as the marketplace and business aspects. In addition, you may need to learn how to build fences and enclosures and determine how many sheep can be kept per acre.

Shepherds must be familiar with dog laws and training, differences in nutritional needs among rams, ewes, and lambs, and subtle signs of illness. Among the latter, foot rot, conjunctivitis, colds, pneumonia, and white muscle disease are but a few, although some vaccinations are available. Sheep are easily lead and will eat anything, even poisonous plants and trash, so you and your dog are the brains of the outfit.

Breeding and birthing patterns can also be tricky, particularly since a lamb is often born in the middle of the night and sometimes comes out backward. You'll also be shearing the sheep, which can be a bad experience for both of you, unless you follow the proper techniques. Preparing the wool for market and the sheep for their eventual transformation into lamb chops are other aspects to consider. Sheep can also be shown at fairs and 4-H clubs, always good training for aspiring shepherds.

You'll need to know what to look for in a healthy sheep (a full set of teeth, steady gait, large, well-proportioned body, fluffy fleece, etc.) as well as how to breed your existing flock to its best potential. Money can be made through selling stock, produce, wool, sheepskins, ram rental, cheese from sheep's milk, even in livestock dog breeding. Your income depends upon how much effort you are willing to expend.

You can do the Mary thing and have one little lamb or start with a small flock. In the long run, sheep can be a whole lot cheaper than a lawn mower; they'll graze on just about any land. And not many jobs allow you to make money woolgathering.

Associations

American Sheep Industry Association
6911 Yosemite Street
Englewood, CO 80112
303/771-3500

Lamb Committee, c/o National Live Stock and Meat Building
444 N. Michigan
Chicago, IL 60611
312/467-5520

National Wool Marketing Corporation
3900 Groves Road
Columbus, OH 43232
614/863-3716

Books

Approved Practices in Sheep Production. Juergenson, Elwoood. Danville, IL: Interstate, 1981.

An Introduction to Keeping Sheep. Upton, Jane and Soden, Dennis. Alexandria Bay, NY: Diamond Farm, nd.

Raising Sheep the Modern Way. Simmons, Paula. Pownal, VT: Storey Communications, 1989.

Sheep and Wool. Botkin, M.P., et al. Englewood, Cliffs, NJ: Prentice-Hall, 1988.

The Shepherd's Guidebook. Bradbury, Margaret. Emmaus, PA: Rodale, 1977.

Magazines

National Wool Grower
Sheep!
Sheep Breeder
The Shepherd
Southern Sheep Producer

Roger High
Shepherd

"Ohio State has one football coach and one shepherd," observes Roger High, who has held the latter title for several years. He started out as an undergraduate at the OSU farm properties a few blocks away from a bustling suburb of Columbus. Today he manages a flock of about one hundred ewes, lambs, and rams as well as several students.

"Our purpose is to educate students in sheep management and give them hands-on experience," he says. "We also do genetic research and study nutrition, fertility, and other medical issues."

High recognizes each of the purebred Suffolk and Dorset sheep by sight. "But I don't get attached to them." Since they only live a few years, he's also raised many of their parents, "and I'll probably know their grandchildren," he says, "as long as I stay around." Still, the sheep are tagged with numbers.

Shepherding can be as simple as walking in front of the flock (not behind it) to lead them, and as complex as the latest computer program for scheduling care based on the desired lambing date. "Since I grew up on a sheep farm, this is the best of both worlds."

Smoke Jumper

Any questions about the danger of this occupation can be answered by the Storm King Mountain fire in Colorado, a 1994 conflagration that destroyed over two thousand acres and killed fourteen smoke jumpers and other personnel. With a base pay of about $9.50 an hour, and no personal health insurance or other benefits (except for overtime and an additional 25 percent hazard pay during a fire), it's anybody's guess what motivates someone to enter this hot spot. However, most smoke jumpers don't care what color your parachute is, as long as it's properly packed with the necessary firefighting equipment.

Even qualifying for this job is a physical feat. Along with having at least two years of firefighting and forestry-related experience, you must be able to run a minimum of 1.5 miles in less than eleven minutes and be able to perform twenty-five pushups, forty-five situps, and seven pull-ups, the latter of which can be extremely difficult for those with limited upper body strength. These are the U.S. Forest Service standards; Bureau of Land Management requirements are even stricter. And you are retested annually.

First-year rookie training includes being yelled at by your superiors, running and doing calisthenics several hours a day, learning how to carry a 110-pound backpack three miles in less than ninety minutes, and, as a bonus, jumping from a forty-foot tower. Are we having fun yet?

However, there is a reason for this apparent madness. The nine main smoke jumper bases near remote areas of the western United States and Alaska serve as the first line of defense against forest fires. Droughts and warm weather bring on the "season," often the result of lightning storms.

Smoke jumpers travel by airplane and jump by parachute near the blaze. They wear fireproof, padded suits to avoid injury and can rappel from a tree with a 150-foot rope carried in their leg pockets. Using the latest equipment and techniques, they often contain fires with a minimum of damage, saving millions of dollars and thousands of acres and lives, both human and animal.

After quickly collecting their cargo (sleeping bags, first aid kits, flares, food, ice for drinking water, gear for climbing trees to retrieve parachutes), they utilize cross-cut or chain saws and sometimes explosives, if, for example, a huge tree has been downed. In larger conflagrations, they "fight fire with fire" by intentionally lighting fires when the wind is favorable. Before they leave, however, all flames must be quieted, ashes stirred to make sure no new blaze pops up, and the area doused with water that is dropped from airlifted tanks or carted from a nearby source.

Stays can be overnight or for many days, depending on the intensity of the fire. Additional smoke jumpers from other bases and other specialized personnel are brought in if the fire continues to spread. Off-road fire trucks, helicopters that dump water on "hot" areas, and fixed-wing bombers that spread flame retardant provide additional support.

Smoke jumpers often fill in the slower seasons November through May by teaching, logging, or hitting the beaches and surfing in the cool water. And when they're not battling blazes, they load equipment, get it ready for the next emergency, repair their parachutes, and assemble other gear. So along with being fit and brave, they must also know how to sew.

Associations

International Association of Fire Fighters
1750 New York Ave.
Washington, DC 20006
202/737-8484

U.S. Department of the Interior
Bureau of Land Management
National Interagency Fire Center
3833 S. Development Ave.
Boise, ID 83705-5354
208/387-5437

U.S. Department of Agriculture
Forest Service
201 14th Street, SW
Washington, DC 20250
202/205-1760

Books

Essentials of Fire Fighting. International Fire Service Training Association. Stillwater, OK: Fire Protection Publications, 1992.
The Fire Chief's Handbook. Casey, James F., ed. New York: Fire Engineering, 1987.
Firefighting Principles and Practices. Clark, William E. New York: Fire Engineering/Penwell, 1991.

Magazines

American Fire Journal
Fire Control Digest
Fire Safety Journal
Professional Fire Fighter

Kasey Rose
Smoke Jumper

Not only is Kasey Rose outnumbered about forty to one in a male-dominated arena, but she admits she's afraid of heights. Still, determination and hard work helped the Boise,

Idaho–based smoke jumper overcome this and other obstacles. "At first, there was resentment and the feeling that I was breaking into something," she says of her present assignment, where she has the distinction of being the female who's lasted the longest. "But now they appreciate the diversity a woman adds to the organization."

Although it's not a requirement, most smoke jumpers are college educated. "A lot of us were trained for something else, and found this instead of a 'real job,'" she laughs. "Each of us is independent and confident and has his or her own way of doing things. But when you spend six months together, you develop a lot of team pride and camaraderie." Rose and the others are often called to Alaska to fight fires. "All that time away can be hard on outside relationships."

Each fire is different, and that's what keeps them jumping. "The average age is thirty-four, but we have a man who's fifty-five. You go into a situation not knowing what's going to develop. That's part of the challenge."

> Who thinks the law has anything to do with justice? It is what we have because we can't have justice.
>
> —WILLIAM MCLLVANNY

Law and Order

Accident Reconstructor
Alarm Systems Consultant
Bail Bond Agent/Bounty Hunter
Driver's License Tester and Driving Instructor
Polygrapher
Private Investigator
Process Server

Accident Reconstructor

This is one job where everything happens by design. Hired by law enforcement agencies, insurance companies, lawyers, or private investigators, accident reconstructors are responsible for determining what occurred and who or what is at fault.

Most are employed by local police departments and are specially trained in engineering, mathematics, and physics. They take several hundred hours of classroom and field-related exercises; such courses are available at several universities throughout the United States. Not all accident reconstructors come from a police background, but most have a degree either in engineering or physics.

They arrive on the scene shortly after the occurrence of a serious or fatal accident and collect evidence, measuring skid marks, making sketches and videotapes, taking photographs, and interviewing witnesses. Although the victims of the accident are often on their way to the hospital or morgue, there is usually still a lot of blood, glass, and hysteria. Accident reconstructors must be precise, analytical, and objective: If a mashed squirrel makes you queasy and teary-eyed, this is not the job for you.

Reports are obtained from medical examiners, hospital records, and living victims. Reconstructors often return to accident scenes to locate any additional witnesses. They examine the vehicles involved, noting the condition of the brakes, dents, and other mechanical reactions. From this data, they can determine how damage occurred, along with the estimated speed and direction of travel, point of impact, even whether or not the turn signal was deployed. Other factors involved include perception and reaction times of drivers, road conditions, obstructions to vision, sign dimensions, engineering hazards, and blood alcohol level, if applicable.

This is where independent reconstructors, usually retained by the defense or insurance companies, come in. They have access to the police and other reports and make their own conclusions from the findings. They independently check things out, talking to witnesses and related parties. There may be conflicting results, particularly if the investigator is hired by the defendant's lawyer. Then even more digging into the evidence is required. In the end, someone is usually designated as responsible, and, if it's the driver, he may lose his license, pay a fine, or go to prison.

Independent reconstructors make excellent money, about $65 an hour minimum, compared to their police brethren who hover around $40,000 a year. However, freelance work isn't as steady, and losing too many cases can hurt business. It's not easy fighting city hall, especially when they got there first.

Associations

Academy of Criminal Justice Sciences: Secretariat
Northern Kentucky University
402 Nunn Hall
Highland Heights, KY 41076
606/572-5634

American Society of Criminology
Ohio State University Research
1314 Kinnear Road, Suite 212
Columbus, OH 43212
216/292-9207

National Council on Crime and Delinquency
685 Market Street, No. 620
San Francisco, CA 94105
415/896-6223

Books

Beyond the Crime Lab. Zonderman, Jon. New York: Wiley, 1990.
Careers in Law Enforcement and Security. Cohen, Paul and Shari. New York: Rosen, 1990.
Criminal Investigation. Palmiotto, Michael J. Chicago: Nelson-Hall, 1994.
Opportunities in Law Enforcement and Justice Careers. Stinchcomb, James. Lincolnwood, IL: NTC, 1990.

Traffic Accident Analysis and Roadway Visibility. Washington, DC: Transportation Research Board, 1988.

Magazines

Criminology
Journal of Criminal Justice
Journal of Forensic Sciences
Law and Order
National Centurion

Dave Johnson
Accident Investigation Officer

With a background as a paramedic, Dave Johnson of the San Jose, California police department has seen his share of grisly collisions. In the event of misdemeanor, hit-and-run, and fatal accidents, he and others show up on the scene in a minivan equipped with videocameras, photographic gear, and other investigative tools. "If I'm on call, I go, even in the middle of the night."

Johnson derives satisfaction from seeing repeat offenders punished, particularly if they fork over large amounts of cash to hire independent reconstructors. "One man who was convicted several times on DWI charges paid an investigative company twenty-five thousand dollars to introduce reasonable doubt. There was a mistrial, and the DA tried again. This time the defendant went to prison."

Johnson foresees a keyless system whereby people will not be able to start their cars unless they've been cleared through a computer database. "It smacks of Big Brother, but it would keep reckless drivers off the road." It might mean less accident reconstruction, but that would suit him just fine.

Alarm Systems Consultant

In today's crime-ridden society, more and more people are turning to electronic protection. The $6.5-billion private security industry is expected to grow about 15 percent a year. That's good news for alarm systems consultants.

As a consultant, you visit homes and businesses and recommend a system that best suits the customer. You need to ascertain the client's security vulnerabilities and concerns—nighttime break-ins, employee theft, industrial espionage—and based on extensive knowledge of each piece of security equipment, determine the type of system needed. This can range from elaborate TV, electronic, and audio surveillance to a relatively simple setup involving contacts and motion detectors.

Requirements for a company that relies heavily on computers differ from those for a retail operation in a shopping mall. And you should gauge how much protection homeowners think they can afford before offering them a system that might be beyond their means.

There are several large alarm corporations: ADT, Brink's, and Westinghouse, as well as smaller local firms. It's best to start out with a well-established company that has a private license (a requirement in most states) and is approved by the Better Business Bureau.

Consultants can come from a variety of backgrounds. Some have done police work, others have a master's degree, still others a high school equivalent education. They are trained in the specifics of the particular system by their employer. But since alarms are constantly being updated and the competition's services may rival or improve upon your company's, you should also be conversant with the latest techniques. Much of this information can be found in industry publications and through talking to other professionals.

What all successful consultants share is the ability to sell. Most earnings come from commission, so you spend the first several months of the job "cold calling" customers in heavy break-in areas and making yourself known to other potential clients, such as upper- and middle-class homeowners and businesses with little or no security.

Initial pickings may be slim, but if you do the job right, customers will start referring their friends and business associates to you. Salaries aren't bad to begin with: $18,000 to $25,000 for the first year or so, up to over $60,000 annually.

But don't be surprised when you hear from a prospect who turned you down the first time. He's just been burglarized and wishes he'd had that alarm system yesterday. But tomorrow at 6:00 A.M. will be just fine.

Associations

International Association of Professional Security Consultants
13819-G Walsingham Road, Suite 350
Largo, FL 34644
813/596-6696

International Security Management Association
105 Charles Street, Suite 280
Boston, MA 02114
800/368-1894

National Burglar and Fire Alarm Association
7101 Wisconsin Ave.
Bethesda, MD 20814
301/907-3202

Security Industry Association
1801 K Street, NW
Washington, DC 20006
202/466-7420

Books

Basic Alarm Electronics. Sanger, John. Boston: Butterworth, 1988.

Design and Application of Security/Fire-Alarm Systems. Traister, John E. New York, McGraw-Hill, 1990.

Security Consulting. Sennewald, Charles. Boston: Butterworth, 1989.

Security and Loss Prevention. Purpura, Philip. Boston: Butterworth-Heinemann, 1991.

Understanding and Servicing Alarm Systems. Trimmer, William H. Boston: Butterworth-Heinemann, 1990.

Magazines

Journal of Security Administration
Security Management
Security World

Dan Anderson
Security Consultant

"You need to be a self-starter," according to Dan Anderson of Westinghouse Security Systems in Baltimore, Maryland. "How well you do is directly related to how much time you put into this job." For him, that means stopping by someone's home or business at 8 P.M., if that's what is convenient for the customer."

Anderson also asks his clients a lot of questions. "The most important thing is finding out what they want. Westinghouse offers systems from ninety-five dollars to ten thousand dollars, so we can accommodate just about anyone.

"I try to provide alternatives. If someone doesn't like the looks of a wire, we can talk about a wireless system. If the home has a pet, then we program an "alley" in the motion detector, so the animal won't set off the alarm. We want people to make informed decisions."

Bail Bond Agent/Bounty Hunter

Forget most of what you've read in crime novels and seen on TV: This is a business first, with requisite codes of behavior, speech, and dress. Not only must you be knowledgeable about state and local laws, but should you work in other states as a bounty hunter, you'll need to be familiar with their legislation as well. Otherwise *you* may end up in jail for not following police procedures while the fugitive goes free.

Some states allow anyone to call himself a bond agent, while others require extensive training, a certification examination, and a background investigation. Independent bond agents post cash or property to bail someone out of jail, while agents under contract with a surety insurance company pledge the company's assets by attaching a limited power of attorney to the bond. Either way, the agent receives a nonrefundable premium (a percentage of the bond amount for services rendered) and collateral (house, cars, etc.) to be held in trust to offset losses should the defendant fail to keep his part of the bargain. If the person leaves town or skips the court date, the agent is responsible for the entire bond, a sum usually in the thousands of dollars.

Here is where bounty hunters (or bail enforcement agents, as they prefer to call themselves) come in. They are responsible for bringing the fugitive back for the trial, and if they succeed, they collect a prearranged sum, often a percentage of the premium. If they fail, they get nothing and if they harm the prisoner, they themselves can be subject to criminal prosecution. Many times the bond agent will go after the fugitive himself.

There are no real prerequisites for bounty hunters, although nearly all are employed (and screened carefully) by a bonding agent or insurance company. The surest way not to get hired is to stroll into an agent's office with a Hell's Angels T-shirt, torn jeans, and a sawed-off shotgun. Most agencies are looking for streetwise, physically fit men and women who blend in with whomever they're dealing and outsmart rather than overpower the criminal.

People usually break into these fields by working with an experienced private detective, bond agent, or bounty hunter. They take courses in criminal investigation at local colleges and read books about techniques of surveillance, arrest, and other aspects of criminal apprehension and legislation. They develop a network of contacts at various utility companies, government agencies, and within the police community to help them track down their quarry.

Should they have to utilize force, they are conversant with physical methods that rarely involve firearms (dogs are often more fearsome). Most bond jumpers come along peacefully. They are not, after all, mass murderers or serial killers. Although agents do carry guns, they can use them legally only in cases of self-defense or to protect another from severe harm or death.

Bond agents with several employees can clear anywhere from $35,000 to $200,000 a year, depending on the number of forfeitures. Most agents-for-hire make approximately $40,000 per annum, while bounty hunters' salaries can vary mightily. Often the latter find it most cost-effective to round up several suspects in a specific geographic area.

Although you may find yourself chasing suspects and climbing fences, much of the work involves talking to and persuading others to go along with you—either as prisoners or in providing information about your quarry. And once you get a line on the suspect, you must keep after him until you've either found him or the trail reaches a dead end, so work runs into evenings, weekends, and may involve eighteen-hour days.

Associations

National Association of Bail Enforcement Agents
P.O. Box 3990
Santa Barbara, CA 93130
(no phone)

Books

Bail Enforcer. Burton, Bob. Boulder, CO: Paladin, 1990.
How to Find Anyone Anywhere. Thomas, Ralph D. Austin, TX: Thomas, nd.
Know Your Rights. Katz, Lewis. Cleveland: Banks-Baldwin, 1993.
Modern Day Bounty Hunting. Mollison, David. Winter Garden, FL: D & G, 1993.
Shadowing and Surveillance: A Complete Guidebook. Rapp, Burt. Port Townsend, WA: Loompanics, nd.
Undercover Work: A Complete Handbook. Rapp, Burt. Port Townsend, WA: Loompanics, 1986.

Magazines

Full Disclosure
Surveillant
Acquisitions for Intelligence Professionals
Crime Control Digest
National Missing Persons Report
Search and Seizure Law Report

David Mollison
Bail Bond Agent/Enforcer

David Mollison of Sorrento, Florida, was in pre-med before he made his dramatic career move. "I've always been fascinated by detective work," he relates. "I decided to become a private investigator and found I was successful at locating missing persons." The logical next step was to open a bond agency: "But it was nonstop. Not only was I responsible for several agents but also for millions of dollars in liabilities." Now he operates on his own.

When Mollison goes into another state to capture someone, he's very careful. "You need to follow procedures and not offend the local authorities. And you must always have the proper paperwork to back yourself up."

Tracking down sources represents another challenge. Not only must he sometimes pay for information "but you need to be careful in interviewing people. Sometimes they'll lie, so it's up to you to figure out the truth."

Mollison says he treats everyone with respect, "even though some suspects do threaten me. But I let them know I'm not intimidated." Just in case, however, he maintains an unlisted home address and phone number.

Driver's License Tester and Driving Instructor

These jobs require nerves of steel and the patience of Job. License testers represent the last barrier between the embryonic driver and freedom. So you will be approached with a great deal of trepidation.

It's up to you to make the client feel at ease, even if you're as anxious as he is. (Will the foreign gentleman understand not to mow down a pedestrian, even though in his country he thinks he has the right of way? Will the teenager be so rattled that she slams on the gas pedal instead of the brakes, taking you with her over the curb and into a plate-glass window?) Because such situations can occur, you must be able to think and act quickly, even if it means seizing control of the car.

As a tester, you'll be responsible for insuring that drivers meet state requirements. This may include running a National Driver Record computer check on out-of-state licenses to make sure they are valid and contain no serious vehicular infractions. You may also be assigned to coordinate and grade the written test for learners' permits.

If you're taking someone out on a test, you'll likely utilize a grade sheet based on a manual of your state's driving requirements. Most tests are divided into two parts: driving and maneuverability. The latter is easier to grade, because either the driver makes it through the cones or he doesn't. He will fail if he knocks over one or two cones, depending upon the regulation.

The road test requires more interpretation. Some testers go "by the book" while others are more lenient. As long as the person seems to have a knowledge of the basics (even if he flips his turn signals a few seconds too soon or too late), he passes. If the driver is comfortable with you, he'll likely do better, even if you're on the strict side.

Upon return to the testing site, you compute the grade, providing constructive criticism about strengths and weaknesses. If you're a stickler or if the driver has messed up, a few tissues might come in handy.

Related to (but completely different from) testers are driving instructors. Representing the front line of safety, they must be excellent drivers themselves and able to instill confidence in even the most timid students. Although requirements are minimal (high school education, clean driving record), they are trained on the job and watched carefully to make sure they communicate well with their students and properly explain concepts.

Pay for instructors hovers around $6 an hour, while testers earn nearly twice as much. The latter are also trained on site, and start out studying manuals, answering phones, and scheduling appointments. Then you go on the road with an examiner who provides coaching and compares his test results with yours to make sure they're compatible.

Minimum requirements for testers are a high school education as well as experience or training in personnel relations, interviewing, and especially mathematics. Should you make a mistake in addition or subtraction, you might inadvertently break someone's heart or accidentally let a menace loose on the road.

Associations

American Driving and Traffic Safety Education Association
Highway Safety Center
R&P Building, IUP
Indiana, PA 15705
412/357-4051

Driving School Association of America
111 W. Pomona Blvd.
Monterary Park, CA 91754
213/728-2100

North American Professional Driver Education Association
5180 N. Elson Ave.
Chicago, IL 60630
312/777-9605

Books

Digest of Motor Laws. Falls Church, VA: AAA, nd.

A History of Driver Education in the United States. Stack, Herbert. Washington, DC: National Commission on Safety Education, 1966.

Learn to Drive. Hensel, George. New York: Warner, 1987.

A Resource Curriculum in Driver and Traffic Safety Education. East Lansing, MI: Michigan State University, 1975.

Associations

American Driving and Traffic Safety Education Association
Highway Safety Center
R&P Building, IUP
Indiana, PA 15705
412/357-4051

Driving School Association of America
111 W. Pomona Blvd.
Monterary Park, CA 91754
213/728-2100

North American Professional Driver Education Association
5180 N. Elson Ave.
Chicago, IL 60630
312/777-9605

Books

Digest of Motor Laws. Falls Church, VA: AAA, nd.
A History of Driver Education in the United States. Stack, Herbert. Washington, DC: National Commission on Safety Education, 1966.
Learn to Drive. Hensel, George. New York: Warner, 1987.
A Resource Curriculum in Driver and Traffic Safety Education. East Lansing, MI: Michigan State University, 1975.
Seat Belts Required. Tatnall, Henry. Pittsburgh: Dorrance, 1993.

Magazines

Driving Instruction
Drive
Driver Trainer Newsletter
Highway Safety Literature
Traffic Safety

Michelle Wallace
License Tester

Michelle Wallace of Columbus, Ohio, worked in the security office of a highway patrol academy before her current job. "It was lonely," she admits. "I wanted something different and to be around people."

Boy, did she get her wish. "This job requires a sense of humor. We took a training course in how to handle the public because you must deal with all types." Teenagers are good drivers, she finds, although she has difficulties with people who don't speak English. "You tell them to do something and get a blank stare. That's scary."

Wallace understands how intimidating it can be for someone to take a driving test. "Because we wear uniforms, people think we're the police. But we're state employees and want to see good drivers pass."

Polygrapher

In this job, you honestly need a split personality. You must be a sensitive interviewer, highly attuned to the responses of your subject, and you must also be a dogmatic interrogator who can pinpoint a fib.

Polygraphs—aka lie detectors—measure slight variations in body functions that signal emotional reactions. The basic machine is a metal box with three to six (usually four) instrument panels, each with an attached pen that independently records a pattern of psychological/physiological responses on a moving chart; and a blood pressure cuff for measuring responses. Answers are checked against "benchmark" questions with obvious replies like name and address.

dropped from over 600 during the 1980s to only about 250 today.

Nevertheless, there is still a need to eliminate or confirm suspects in law enforcement. Tests are also utilized by lawyers to help construct a defense, as well as to determine whether sexual and other offenders have violated parole or probation. Results are sometimes ruled admissible in court. And Uncle Sam still gives tests to certain categories of employees.

To the average person, polygraphy has the taint of a stark room with a single chair dominated by a cigar-smoking detective. So don't be offended if your subjects seem none too happy to see you.

Associations

American Association of Police Polygraphers
1918 Sleepy Hollow
Pearland, TX 77581-5740
713/485-0902

American Polygraph Association
Suite 800, 5700 Building
P.O. Box 8037
Chattanooga, TN 37411-4015
800/272-8037

Books

The Complete Polygraphy Handbook. Abrams, Stan. Lexington, MA: D.C. Heath, 1989.

The Lie Detection Book. Majeski, William J. and Ralph Butler. New York: Ballantine, 1988.

Lie Detector Use in the Workplace. Tulcaz, Gary. Paramus, NJ: Prentice-Hall, 1992.

Magazines

Polygraph
American Association of Police Polygraph Journal
Journal of Polygraph Science

Harry Ortiz
Polygrapher

Harry Ortiz of Corpus Christi, Texas, has seen a lot of changes since 1982 when he became a licensed polygrapher. "We're using polygraphy more in the courts and in the justice system," he observes. "It's becoming accepted by psychologists and social workers."

There is a movement afoot to standardize licensing and add to educational requirements so all are trained and tested in basically the same manner. "So far," says Ortiz, "only about twenty-five states require licensing."

He tries to make the testing as mentally painless to the subject as possible and takes great care to appear innocuous and unassuming. "If they're not comfortable, then I won't get good results. It's my job to allay their fears without interfering."

Private Investigator

First of all, you can forget Sam Spade. Much of this job involves sitting—in cars, in someone's office, in front of the computer—and asking a lot of questions. And on a *really* exciting day, you might get to sift through someone's garbage for clues as to their whereabouts or activities. This is a field where you need to develop many contacts and cultivate favors, because you never know when you'll need information from an obscure source. So it pays to be nice to everyone.

Also—unlike Sam Spade—you can get much farther by acting normal and blending in than by skulking around in a trench coat. People will more likely open up to you—even if they tell you lies. Other personal requirements include objectivity, logic, perseverance, good communications skills, a strong sense of ethics, knowledge of the law, and keen powers of observation. The latter two come in especially handy if a subject has caught on to your surveillance and decides to confront you as you round the corner. And it helps to be a bit of a ham so you can invent various identities and pretexts as the situation arises.

Unlike the terrified and desperate individuals (usually women) depicted on TV and in the movies, clients are more likely to be law firms and insurance companies needing someone to locate witnesses and secure evidence; governmental agencies wanting background checks on employees; and corporations looking to uncover theft, industrial espionage, and other white-collar crimes. Still, even these jobs require mastery of investigative techniques such as roping (obtaining information without raising witnesses' suspicions), pretexts, surveillance, interrogations, "locates" (finding a subject), background investigations, and undercover operations. These same techniques also come in handy during domestic cases when one partner is suspicious of the other, and in finding skip tracers who have seemingly disappeared.

Despite popular myth, the private investigator (PI) is not considered a law enforcement official. Yet while operating (barely) within the confines of the law, a PI sometimes obtains false IDs, picks locks, "snoops" via photography and videotape, utilizes electronic surveillance such as bugs, and gets restricted information through almost any means except violence. This requires skill, subtlety, and a knack for not getting caught.

Few would attempt to learn this job on their own, and although criteria differ with each vicinity, most states require that you first work with a licensed PI agency. Some home courses are available, but established professionals recommend college classes in photography, psychology, legal procedures, government, criminology, law enforcement, business, and computers. And a university degree will lend credibility to your business.

likely to be law firms and insurance companies needing someone to locate witnesses and secure evidence; governmental agencies wanting background checks on employees; and corporations looking to uncover theft, industrial espionage, and other white-collar crimes. Still, even these jobs require mastery of investigative techniques such as roping (obtaining information without raising witnesses' suspicions), pretexts, surveillance, interrogations, "locates" (finding a subject), background investigations, and undercover operations. These same techniques also come in handy during domestic cases when one partner is suspicious of the other, and in finding skip tracers who have seemingly disappeared.

Despite popular myth, the private investigator (PI) is not considered a law enforcement official. Yet while operating (barely) within the confines of the law, a PI sometimes obtains false IDs, picks locks, "snoops" via photography and videotape, utilizes electronic surveillance such as bugs, and gets restricted information through almost any means except violence. This requires skill, subtlety, and a knack for not getting caught.

Few would attempt to learn this job on their own, and although criteria differ with each vicinity, most states require that you first work with a licensed PI agency. Some home courses are available, but established professionals recommend college classes in photography, psychology, legal procedures, government, criminology, law enforcement, business, and computers. And a university degree will lend credibility to your business.

Before opening their doors, independent operators will likely undergo a police background check and will need a surety bond or liability insurance and a business license. Then, given enough experience, they can start charging between $25 and $100 per day, eventually working their way into a comfortable living.

And you'd best document your activities: Telling a client he owes you one thousand dollars for a futile search without a detailed report might result in him investigating *you*.

Magazines

Clues: Journal of Detection
Investigators
Master Detective Magazine
P.I. Magazine
Scientific Sleuthing Newsletter

John Bailey
Private Investigator

After over ten years as a PI, John Bailey of Klamath Falls, Oregon prefers operating from his office. "I've been attacked doing security work, pulled a black bag job to get information in a divorce case, and done my share of sitting in a hot car and dumpster diving," he says. "It's easier and more lucrative for me to make phone calls and do computer research."

Still, Bailey believes PIs should start out with the so-called dirty work and favors. "It's the best way to develop necessary skills and contacts. I knew I was getting somewhere when lawyers I worked for began taking me to restaurants I normally couldn't afford."

He likens his job to that of a computer technician who gets paid a bundle for pushing the right button. "It may seem simple, but you need to know exactly where to look."

Process Server

This is one "service" job where you can lose a few teeth if you're not careful. Most people aren't exactly thrilled when you, a total stranger, walk up to them and hand them a piece of paper telling them they must appear in court. This is especially true when this is done around their friends, coworkers, or family.

Along with understanding the requirements of the law and correct procedures, process servers must have a good grasp of human nature. They must make sure their dress and demeanor fit in with the surroundings, whether they're delivering flowers (along with the summons or subpoena) or infiltrating a country club to get to a rich executive surrounded by bodyguards. They must be subtle, businesslike, and very quick. If they mess up, the serve can be quashed, and they themselves may be hauled into court to determine whether the serve was properly executed.

Many circumstances, however, are routine. Clients tend to be lawyers and summonses and subpoenas can involve anything from a dissolution of marriage to a lawsuit, to complex criminal cases. And by their very nature, legal situations engender lots of paperwork, so a case usually involves several summonses. For instance, a personal injury lawsuit for an automobile accident may require the court appearance of the police officers of record; the doctors, nurses, and attendants at the hospital where the victims were brought; witnesses; the tow truck operator; even fire fighters.

In a few states, just about any U.S. citizen over the age of eighteen can serve process. However, most require that you be certified or registered within a certain judicial district and carry a surety bond protecting the state. Depending upon the type of paper being served (i.e., summons, subpoena, injunction), licensed private investigators and bail bond agents may also qualify.

In recent years, computers have greatly simplified the tracking down of individuals. It's frighteningly easy to trace someone and obtain an address from a driver's license and credit records. As a result, more people with less training are working as process servers, and rates have plummeted, in the South Florida area, for example, from an average of $25 a serve and 35 cents a mile in the eighties to $12 a serve with no mileage, today.

Those working for an agency make about $15,000 to $18,000 per annum, while the self-employed realize more, because the cases they take on are usually more difficult and involve research and travel expenses.

On the plus side, there will never be a shortage of customers.

Associations

National Association of Private Process Servers
P.O. Box 8202
Northfield, IL 60093
312/973-7712

National Association of Professional Process Servers
P.O. Box 4547
Portland, OR 97208
800/477-8211

See also entries for Bail Bond Agent/Bounty Hunter and Private Detective.

Books

Defense and Control Tactics. Sylvain, Georges. Englewood Cliffs, NJ: Prentice-Hall, 1971.

Due Process of Law. Gora, Joel. Skokie, IL; National Textbook, 1977.

The Ratification of the Fourteenth Amendment. James, Joseph B. Macon, GA: Mercer University, 1984.

Magazines

The Docket Street
Comprehensive Verdict Service

Lyman and Ellen Bradford
Process Servers

For the Bradfords of West Palm Beach, Florida, process serving is a family affair. Lyman and Ellen are now training their eighteen-year-old son Lyman IV in the basics. "Part of this is learning how to conduct skip traces," observes the senior Lyman, who used to be a private investigator. "It's the same as working on a missing persons case. You pull out all the stops and do whatever it takes to locate someone."

Also, "you have to be able to tell when someone is lying. People will deny their identities if they don't want to be served." Bradford isn't afraid to take risks. "One man was going through a nasty divorce, and had a reputation for knocking people out. I geared myself up, walked into his home, and stuck the divorce papers right under his armpit. By the time he realized what had happened, I was gone."

The fact that someone has money doesn't necessarily make the job easier. "In a place like Palm Beach, there are more layers of people—security guards, maids—between yourself and the person you're serving."

Acting is all about honesty. If you can fake that, you've got it made.

—GEORGE BURNS

Let Us Entertain You

Clown
Film Extra
Model
Music Teacher
Singing Telegram
Square Dance Caller

Clown

While clowning seems to come naturally to some individuals, it isn't as easy as it looks. Why else would Ringling Bros. and Barnum & Bailey circus have a clown college? And make the tuition *free*? (Although those who are accepted must pay room and board, a materials fee, and provide their own transportation and spending money.)

In order to be a successful clown, you must master the fine arts of balloon twisting, face makeup, pantomine, and assorted gags. Ringling's Baraboo, Wisconsin, Clown College ("the only institution in the world solely dedicated to [this] ancient and honorable art," according to its promotional materials) also offers a curriculum "rich in juggling, pie-throwing, and stilt walking" as well as the more serious pursuits of costume construction, prop building, arena choreography, improvisation, and acrobatics. At the end of an intensive eight-week training period, the "fledgling funsters" audition for a spot in the circus.

Those accepted will find the pay low and the lifestyle spartan. However, in return they get to see the world (at the very least, most of the lower forty-eight states) and meet and work with fascinating people. On the road eleven months out of the year, many circus clowns are single and in their twenties.

However, you don't have to get your master's in mirth to start clowning around. Instruction can also be found at local clown or magic shops from reputable, experienced clowns who are willing to take on apprentices.

Much employment can be found outside the circus tent. Clowns are in demand for children's birthday parties, corporate events, and promotional tie-ins. These can be quite profitable, ranging from $65 to $75 for a forty-five-minute appearance at a party to $50 an hour for four to six hours of company work. Of course, you must please even the most disruptive child and finicky boss (according to one experienced clown, enlisting the kid's help is a good way of enabling his cooperation, although adults may not be quite so easily enticed). And, although they're not as lucrative, charitable events and local children's TV shows provide excellent exposure and bring joy to the less fortunate.

Clowns starting out will have to spring for their own makeup and props, which can be as little or much as the imagination allows. You can have "live" props, such as dogs, monkeys, and cats, if you can get them to cooperate (see Pet Trainer). You may also find yourself working for free or for a great deal less than the going rate to gain experience. Until they get their big feet wet, many clowns stay employed in their day jobs.

The primary requisite for this field is an ability to make people smile. You may be a Bozo, but everybody loves you.

Associations

Clowns of America
P.O. Box 570
Lake Jackson, TX 77566-0570
409/297-6699

Ringling Bros. and Barnum & Bailey Clown College
8607 Westwood Center Drive
Vienna, VA 22182
703/448-4000

Books

Clown Act Omnibus. McVicar, Wes. Colorado Springs: Meriwether, 1987.
Clown Alley. Ballantine, Bill. Boston: Little, Brown, 1982.
Clown: For Circus and Stage. Stolzenberg, Mark. New York: Sterling, 1983.
Creative Clowning. Fife, Bruce, et al. Bellaire, TX: Java, 1987.
How to Be a Compleat Clown. Sanders, Toby. New York: Stein and Day, 1978.

Magazines

Bandwagon
Calliage
Circus Week
Juggler's World

Uncle Buster
Clown-at-Large

Buster Kern (aka Uncle Buster) of Louisville, Kentucky, truly revels in his second career, which involves entertaining at parties, openings, and for charity. "I was a real estate agent for thirty years and make good money as a clown with a lot less time involved," he says. "But the best reward is when a child comes up to me and tells me I'm doing a good job."

It isn't all funny noses and balloon tricks, though. "Sometimes you stand for hours in all kinds of weather. You need a high level of energy to maintain your character. . . . The last person you encounter is as important as the first." Kern's work can be on evenings and weekends, and may consist of several performances in one day.

Clowns must be especially mindful of how they appear to others. "I let children come over to me and am very careful about physical contact. Even the most innocent gesture can be misconstrued." Only the sincere need apply. "You must genuinely like to make people happy."

Film Extra

These days, movies are hardly magical for film extras in Los Angeles. When their union, the Screen Extras Guild, went under, the Screen Actors Guild (SAG) adopted it like a resentful stepparent. Since then, base pay for a union extra has dropped from $86 to $65 for an eight-hour day (plus overtime and related expenses), making it barely competitive with the nonunion fee of $40 a day. Extras—especially those starting out or nearing retirement age—became unable to meet the miniumum annual income (around $5,000 to $6,000) to obtain health insurance and pension benefits under union rules. Many hover dangerously near the poverty level and are forced to take nonunion work to pay rent and put food on the table. To make matters worse, the folks at SAG are uncooperative and seem to have no interest in improving the situation.

Things look brighter on the other coast, however, and in points between. A totally separate local, SAG in New York, handles union extras in their area but *their* base pay is $90 a day. Rates for smaller cities are comparable.

While some states have no union at all, it's still difficult to become a full-time extra unless you join the union. In some places, a certain quota of union slots must be filled before casting companies turn to nonunion sources. And there is the matter of the aforementioned health and retirement benefits. Other unions include Actor's Equity and the American Federation of Television and Radio Artists (AFTRA) for stage shows and radio/TV jobs, respectively.

Requirements vary for union membership, but usually a speaking part, however small, or three pay vouchers for extra work from a production company guarantee admission. You then pay a one-time initiation fee (around twelve hundred dollars for the SAGs) and yearly dues, which are much less and based on annual SAG income.

Despite these drawbacks, people who become extras claim they find the lifestyle addicting. "You meet a lot of important people," says one veteran. "Even if they don't talk to you, being around them is very exciting."

The job requires tenacity, determination, and a very thick skin. Studios notify casting agencies of their needs (older men, black actors, children age ten to twelve); extras phone the agencies continuously to see if there is any work the following day. They should also always be accessible via beeper or answering service. Some services with unofficial "preferred lists," get information from casting offices and contact extras themselves. So you must call constantly and you need to have a permanent address so checks can be sent to you.

Depending on the production company and the people involved, extras can be treated nasty or nice (the union dictates, however, that they receive meals at certain intervals and be given a place to sit and shelter, if necessary). They are expected to follow directions and understand film lingo. Many also have a usable car—all the better if it's a luxury model—which, if utilized on the set, brings in extra money. They need changes of wardrobe (shabby clothes, formal wear theme and period costumes) to meet the film's requirements. Most important, they should act professional and try to blend into the background, rather than stand out, grinning at Mom and Dad who may be watching from their hometown.

According to experienced extras, the job should be considered an end in itself rather than a stepping-stone to stardom. "There are easier and less time-consuming ways of making money while trying to break in," observes one. For extras, a little must go a long way, especially in Los Angeles.

Associations

Actor's Equity
165 West 46th Street
New York, NY 10036
212/869-8530

American Federation of Television and Radio Artists (AFTRA)
260 Madison Ave.
New York, NY 10016
212/532-0800

Screen Actor's Guild (New York)
1515 Broadway
New York, NY 10036
212/944-1030

In Los Angeles or its environs, look under "Casting services" in the Yellow Pages, the largest of which is:

Central Casting/Cenex
1700 W. Burbank Blvd.
Burbank, CA 91506
818/569-5200

Books

Acting with Style. Harrop, John and Sabin Epstein. New York: Prentice-Hall, 1982.

Back to One. Chambers, Colin. Los Angeles: author, 1992.

Hollywood Extras Manual. Wegner, Robert. Phoenix: author, 1994. (book available only from P.O. Box 31337, Phoenix, AZ 85046).

How to Get Work as a Movie Extra. Worthington, Todd. Seattle: Walk Away Entertainment, 1991.

Opportunities in Acting Careers. Moore, Dick. Lincolnwood, IL: NTC, 1993.

The Samuel French bookstore (7623 Sunset Blvd, Hollywood, CA 90026, 213/876-0570) has a selection of self-published and small press titles.

Magazines

Casting News
Drama-Logue
Faces International
Show Biz News

Faith Burton
Extra/Stand-In

After trying the corporate world and raising two children, Faith Burton of Burbank, California, decided to become an extra. "My ex-husband was a stuntman, so I knew some directors and casting agents." She's seen a lot of changes in her ten years on the job, "most of them negative, which is why a lot of extras have either moved out of this area or quit."

Rather than giving up, Burton became a stand-in for such actresses as Maggie Smith and Lauren Bacall. "The money is *much* better and if a star takes a liking to you and appreciates your work, you can establish a higher base fee." Like the seasoned extra that she is, Burton has a bag of tricks (high heels, wigs) to help her resemble the performer while the crew adjusts the surrounding lighting.

"Being a good extra requires acting skills, such as a silent, intuitive reaction to the camera," she observes. Should directors appreciate your efforts or a cinematographer discover your stand-in talents, you may find yourself with a very small but influential fan club.

Model

Becoming a successful model requires more luck and timing than actual skill or even ambition. Agencies and clients are searching for an emphemeral "look," or whatever fits the trend of the moment. And the road to fame and fortune is littered with the potholes of illegitimate modeling schools and agencies, lecherous and dishonest photographers, and food, drink, and drugs that can ruin figures and careers.

However, understanding these caveats may at least increase your chances of making a living in this tenuous profession. But before various booking agencies will even consider you, you need to act, dress and present youself with care and have a portfolio of professional-quality shots. Reputable modeling schools can provide instruction in poise, elocution, wardrobe, and fitness, and fashion photographers specialize in helping you look attractive and up-to-date in various poses and attire. Either can run into the thousands of dollars so check them out before writing a check. Acting courses at local schools and colleges are also helpful.

Even those who manage to sign with an agency may face disappointment and rejection. You'll make rounds and go-sees, which are basically cattle calls involving dozens of other models like yourself. You may be booked solid for a month, then for no apparent reason, have nothing for several weeks. If you're on an out-of-town assignment or are hired by an agency in a foreign country, you have the added stress of finding your way around in a strange place, among people who may not speak English. And male and female models dressed for an assigment must learn how to deal with stares and unwanted advances.

The profession does have advantages, however. Pay starts at $25 an hour for informal modeling and tops out at between $100 and $250 an hour, even in smaller cities. Of course the so-called superstars earn much much more. And there are a variety of venues, ranging from hand and foot modeling to runway modeling to work that appears in brochures, magazines, on TV commercials, even on billboards. Although the standard requirements for models are youth, slimness, and height, petites, the overweight, and "character types" of all ages, from babies to septugenarians, can find employment. The key is to be flexibile, available, and willing to take on all jobs, as long as they don't involve nudity. (Unless, of course, that's what you want. See also Singing Telegram.)

As a model, it's not your place to make suggestions and provide input, even if you see a more efficient method of doing things. And insulting the client is a surefire way of losing a job. You are expected to be pliable, willing to please, and patient. After all, they're paying you to just sit (or stand or walk) there and look pretty. As long as you act like a professional, the legions waiting to replace you will just have to take a number.

Associations

World Modeling Association
440 San Pedro Drive, NE, No. 801
Albuquerque, NM 87109
505/883-2823

Books

Getting Started in Acting and Modeling. Alexandria, Felicia. Newark, CA: Mystique, 1990.

How to Become a Model. John Fort Studio [videocassette]. Cambridge, WV: Cambridge Career Products, 1991.
Male Modeling. Marlowe, Francine. New York: Crown, 1980.
Modeling Made Easy. Colquitt, Ken. Atlanta: Starmakers, 1988.
The Model's Handbook. Roderick, Kyle. New York: Morrow, 1984.

Magazines

Glamour
Mademoiselle
Model & Performer
Model News
many others

Tara Green
Fashion Model

"When I was fifteen, I was hired by an agency in Milan," recalls Tara Green of Dublin, Ohio. "My mother couldn't come with me because she had to take care of my younger sister. And I knew nothing about being a real model."

When Green arrived, she not only had to cope with sharing a tiny, primitive apartment with several other models but with negotiating her way in a foreign city. "I was running all over the place. It was neither glamorous nor exciting."

She also had to learn how to handle men. "They follow you everywhere. You can't act scared or they'll take it as encouragement." In addition, "at the clubs, models are treated like VIPs and can have all the free food and drinks they want. So it's tempting to stay up and party, even if you have an early morning call."

Still, Green finds modeling rewarding, both financially and personally. "The actual work is the easiest part, and I'm saving money for college. I've found friends and visited places I would have otherwise never experienced."

Music Teacher

Music teachers must have a thorough knowledge of their instrument, be it clarinet, violin, or zither. They must convey information so that even young children understand, and portray an enthusiasm conducive to learning. Many music teachers also entertain at parties and in public places, market their own songs, and give recitals featuring their students.

Those who teach in a public or private school setting usually need a bachelor's degree from an approved teacher training program and may require certification. The median salary for a public school teacher is $36,000 (secondary) and $34,800 (primary). You must be able to deal with reluctant and uninterested students, which can be frustrating to even the most dedicated artist.

Independent instructors have more flexibility and, because they are being paid for a specific service, have a more motivated clientele. You can open a facility on a separate site or give lessons at your home or at the student's home. You can choose to work during regular business hours or on evenings and weekends.

Many musicians become independent teachers after years of professional experience and may bypass postsecondary education altogether. They may want to stay at home and raise a family or find a "real" job and make some actual money while keeping a hand in their chosen field. Teaching can also provide income while they compose music or put together a new act.

Still, unless you're already famous or wealthy, this is not a field that will make you rich. Most teachers charge $15 to $20 per lesson—more if they have a huge following or run a well-known school. Music stores and institutes as well as the local suburban paper are good ways to locate potential students. Once you're established, word of mouth will supply the rest.

Along with making music interesting and enjoyable, you'll need to inspire students to actually *want* to practice those scales again and again when you're not around. You must also be able to organize and direct a recital in which proud parents and friends come to see the prodigy pounding the keys (or sawing the strings).

Most important, music teachers need lots of patience. Because if a student becomes discouraged and alienated, he might end up breaking into a store to steal instruments rather than playing them.

Associations

National Association of Schools of Music
11250 Roger Bacon Drive, Suite 21
Reston, VA 22091
703/437-0700

Music Teacher National Association
441 Vine Street, Suite 505
Cincinnati, OH 45202
513/421-1420

Society for Music Teacher Education
1806 Robert Fulton Drive
Reston, VA 22091
800/336-3738

Books

A Creative Approach to Music Fundamentals. Duckworth, William. Belmont, CA: Wadsworth, 1989.

Education and Music. Fletcher, Peter. New York: Oxford University Press, 1989.
The Muse Within. Bjorkvold, Jon R. New York: HarperCollins, 1992.
Music Mind Games. Yurko, Michiko. Miami: CPP/Belwin, 1992.
A Philosophy of Music Education. Reimer, Bennett. Englewood Cliffs, NJ: Prentice-Hall, 1989.

Magazines

American Music Teacher
Journal of Music Teacher Education
Journal of Research on Music Education
Teaching Music
Today's Music Educator

Chuck Dailey
Guitar Teacher and Composer

A teacher of guitar for over forty-five years, Chuck Dailey of Gahanna, Ohio, has instructed people from age four to eighty. "The basics are the same," he explains "No matter how much education people have, they still must learn how to handle the guitar and play the strings."

At one time, Dailey practically had to turn away youngsters, "but things have changed. Parents can't afford the luxury of outside music lessons." And his clientele has shifted more to adults. "These are people who want to play for fun or to supplement other musical talents." He also markets and sells his own "health and relaxation" tapes. These have been utilized all over the world in hospitals, doctors' offices, and as a aid to increasing concentration.

One of Dailey's greatest rewards is encountering former students. "They work in music stores, for record companies, or as teachers." One young man even ended up on *Star Search* and has a recording contract in Nashville.

"Guitar is something they can do for the rest of their lives," he adds. Teaching keeps Dailey young because he needs to be familiar with the stylings of both Les Paul *and* Metallica.

Singing Telegram

Do you enjoy taking off (some of) your clothes and acting bizarre in front of strangers? Seeing people get embarrassed and flustered by your presence? Singing in a loud but pleasing voice that reaches into the far corners of a room? If the answers are "yes," this may be the job for you.

Singing telegrams are utilized for a number of celebrations (birthdays, anniversaries, promotions) as well as for some not-so-happy purposes like the break up of a relationship or to publicly humiliate someone. As a singing telegram, you may not know what's really going on until you get to your destination and the recipient slams the door in your face or bursts into tears. Despite this, you must keep smiling and deliver the message (through rain, sleet, a keyhole, whatever).

Since most requests are for evenings and weekends, this job is ideal for students, homemakers, or persons looking to supplement their incomes. Although you don't need formal training, acting skills, poise, and stage presence are required. A variety of "schticks" (gorilla, stripper, bag lady) will also increase your employability.

Part-timers (fifteen hours a week) make about $10,000 a year, while those who work twenty-five to thirty hours can easily pull in $20,000. And these figures don't even include tips. Expenses involve a reliable car and attractive costumes, applicable props, and a tape player, if music is involved. Those owning a singing telegram agency can earn much more, but they also have the added responsiblity and overhead of running a small business and therefore need appropriate experience and education.

Your customers expect you to arrive on time and do an approximately fifteen-minute-long presentation tailored to their needs. During the initial contact, you'll be getting information about the recipient to incorporate into your act.

Singing telegrams come from all walks of life, and in all shapes, ages, sizes, and races. And there's a new audience every hour.

Associations

American Guild of Variety Artists
184 5th Ave.
New York, NY 10010
212/675-1003

Association of Comedy Artists
P.O. Box 1796
New York, NY 10025
212/864-6620

Books

Acting Professionally. Cohen, Robert. Mountain View, CA: Mayfield, 1990.
On Performing. Craig, David. New York: McGraw-Hill, 1989.
Performing Your Best. Kubistant, Tom. Champaign, IL: Life Enhancement, 1986.
Stay Home and Star! Steele, William P. Portsmouth, NH: Heinemann, 1992.

Magazines

AGVA News
American Humor
Comic Highlights
The Jokesmith
Just for Laughs

Barbara Shehane
Owner, Eastern Onion

Although she worked as an account representative for Xerox, Barbara Shehane of Kansas City, Kansas, was trained as a musician and sang part-time. So she jumped at the chance to buy the local Eastern Onion franchise. "Owning your own business is great, but also a lot of work," she observes. "Although franchise owners can gross up to $700,000 a year in large cities, you must pay royalties, office and phone expenses, and good salaries to attract quality people."

Shehane delivers many telegrams herself. "It can be stressful. You may have to cross town several times in one night to perform. And if you're even five minutes late, it can throw you off for the entire evening."

But the rewards are worth the demands. "I love making people laugh and helping them forget their troubles. Most everyone gets a kick out of it." Especially the time she went to a bank to appear as the Grim Reaper for a birthday party, and the security guards told her to come out of her car with her hands up. She'd been mistaken for a robber, and this time, the joke was on her.

Square Dance Caller

In order to become a caller, you must first know how to square dance. Western-style square dancing requires weeks of instruction and practice, as well as memorization of sixty-eight basic moves or "figures." And that's just the beginning—accomplished dancers need to know more than four hundred moves. Western-style dancers have a whole subculture, with clubs, a dress code (dresses with petticoats for the ladies, long-sleeved shirts and slacks for men), and conventions. Clubs hold dances at least once a week, more during holidays.

More casual square dancing (Eastern-style) involves "one-night stands" at various private parties and other functions. Because participants may not be familiar with the moves and may be under the influence, the calls must be simple and clear. Nothing's more distracting than having someone stumble over their feet, throwing off the timing of the entire set. Square dancing is highly codependant.

Callers attend "caller colleges," four- or five-day intensive workshops, or else apprentice with experienced callers. You'll learn proper use of microphone and additional equipment, voice delivery and singing techniques, formation management and choreography, timing, and much more. Once you gain experience, you may find yourself "making up" dances (from specific moves) as you go along, rather than following a set pattern of preordained moves. The more fun, original, and challenging the calls, the more calls you'll receive for future gigs.

Pay is good—$80 to $150 a night—and even better for out-of-town callers invited to conventions and other gatherings (several hundred to a few thousand, plus airfare, hotel, and car rental). However, few can make this their sole source of income unless they're at a dude ranch or other resort area. Square dancing occurs mostly on weekend nights, and areas with a high concentration of clubs usually have several callers. Still, callers can pull in additional funds by giving lessons to dancers and training other callers. Proficiency in other types of moves, such as for round dancing and contra, or line, dancing add to marketability.

Start-up expenses involve a microphone, songs, a tape player, and possibly musical instruments. Callers must also get permission to use the music. CALLERLAB (see below) has a resource list of over three million copyrighted tunes approved for most situations. Most callers belong to either CALLERLAB or a local association of callers.

Finally, callers must have a good singing and pleasant speaking voice. You carry the tune, in more ways than one.

Associations

CALLERLAB
829-3rd Ave., SE
Rochester, MN 55904
507/288-5121

National Square Dance Convention
2936 Bella Vista
Midwest City, OK 73110-4199
405/732-0566

United Square Dancers
8913 Seaton Drive
Huntsville, AL 35802
205/861-6044

Books

Honor Your Partners! Square Dances With Calls (audio cassette). Washington, DC: Folkways, 1991.
Square Dances. Pete Piute, caller (audio cassette). Washington, DC: Folkways, 1991.
Square Dances of Today: and How To Teach and Call Them. Kraus, Richard G. New York: Ronald Press, 1950.

Magazines

American Squaredance Magazine
National Square Dance Directory

Grace Wheatley
Square Dance Caller

Sixteen years ago, Grace Wheatley of Gallup, New Mexico, was encouraged by her husband to try what has been traditionally a male-dominated profession. "Women have a different voice range than men, so sometimes dancers are uncomfortable with that," she says. Although there are more women callers today, "the figure is still under 10 percent"

Wheatley had to find records to harmonize with, a challenge since most were geared to men with lower voices. As a result, she made her own recordings, which are utilized all over the world today. She has been invited to square dance festivals around the United States and Canada, and in New Zealand, Australia, and other countries.

"Although it takes up weekends and leisure time, I get to do what I love best in a wholesome atmosphere," she observes. Indeed, she's found her true "calling."

My photographs do me an injustice. They look just like me.

—PHYLLIS DILLER

Photography and Video Buffs

Electronic Media Designer
Holographer
Photo Researcher
Special Occasion Photographer
Videographer

Electronic Media Designer

Video graphics specialists, broadcast designers, electronic media designers, regardless of what they're called, these folks create moving images for television, cable, and film as well as print material, such as advertisements and billboards. Unlike traditional designers, they utilize cutting-edge technology in the form of computers and other equipment. Theirs is a "paperless" medium; programs such as Quantel Paintbox, Digital FX, and others have replaced traditional color guides, typesetting machines, and Exacto knives. The possiblities are infinite, and there's no mess to clean up.

This relatively new field has burgeoned with the increase and widespread use of technology. TV stations, networks, production companies, public relation firms, animation studios, and other visual media enterprises utilize full-time or freelance designers. These people produce network graphics and animation, including logos, opening credits, and titles. They may also pull together commercials, music videos, infomercials, instructional videos, and corporate image promotions. Through computer manipulation, they can make a program out of several existing videos and photographs or create something entirely new and different.

In order to do this, you need a thorough knowledge of a specific medium. For instance, television screens have a fixed resolution and can handle only so much visual input, and colors often appear different on camera than in the original design. You may also work under tight deadlines, creating and changing designs according to the station's schedule, or based on suggestions from higher-ups. This may involve evenings and weekends to accommodate short lead times.

Although colleges do offer courses in computer graphics, only a few schools, such as the Ringling School of Art and Design in Sarasota, Florida (not to be confused with Ringling's Clown College in Baraboo, Wisconsin), provide specific training in television and other media. A background in design and color as well as in lighting and photography is also helpful.

Pay for this field varies widely, from $30,000 to $110,000 a year, depending upon the geographical area and job responsiblities. And designers must be flexibile—employers have their own methods, equipment, and ways of doing things. It also helps to be proficient in as many graphics programs as possible. Those starting out on their own can expect to pay as much as thirty-thousand dollars for even basic apparatus or can work with a less expensive Mac program and rent equipment from an existing shop.

Working this way is as close to instant gratification as an artist can get. And when this group gets together for conventions, they know how to party.

Associations

Broadcast Designers Association (BDA)
470 Park Ave. South, 9th floor
New York, New York 10016
212/251-8712

Institute of Business Designers
1 Design Center Pl.
Boston, MA 02210
617/338-6380

Society of Broadcast Engineers
8445 Keystone Crossing, Suite 140
Indianapolis, IN 46240
317/253-1640

Books

Interaction of Color. Albers, Josef. New Haven, CT: Yale University, 1975.

The New Graphic Designer's Handbook. Campbell, Alastair. Philadelphia: Running Press, 1993.

Also the following titles from BDA (see above for address): *Designing for Television: News Sets* (1980); *Designing for Television: News Graphics* (1981); *Designing for Television: the New Tools* (1983).

Magazines

Cinefax
Diem
Film and Video News
Film Technology News
Sightlines
Liquid Image
TV Technology

Don Novak
Media Designer

When Don Novak of Easton, Connecticut, went to college in the early seventies, none of the equipment he works with today had been invented. "Until the eighties, technology for video graphics was very expensive. There were only a few machines that could manipulate visuals."

Novak graduated in fine arts and came to broadcast design after stints as a carpenter, draftsperson, truck driver, and other jobs. "Then I met a TV crew and started going on location and learned about cameras, engineering, and video in general. The station bought a machine that did graphics and I began working with it."

Today Novak 's employed by a postproduction house, developing coherent videos from raw material. "We add shots for continuity or do close-up zooms for dramatic effect." He has also created animation and logos for television. "You need to grab someone's attention while they're channel surfing. The fun is in making an idea understandable and accessible to viewers."

Holographer

This tripping of the light fantastic has been around only since the 1960s and offers the best of both art and science. An interference phenomenon involving lasers and dependent upon the wave nature of light, holography may be a lot easier to accomplish than fully explain. Let the physicists figure it out.

Holography is utilized in disciplines ranging from medicine to engineering to art to architecture to advertising and entertainment. It can introduce and promote new products, identify employees for security purposes, and pinpoint illnesses for MRIs (magnetic resonance images) and CAT scans, as well as discern diseases through a microscope.

Because it produces three-dimensional representations down to molecular exactness, holography can also be quite beautiful as an independent art form. Advances in film, photochemistry, lasers, power sources, and equipment in general have contributed to its increasingly widespread use.

Those who wish to become holographers need only a high school education, along with a background in physics, engineering, photography, and the arts. Lest this sound too intimidating, there are several schools of holography, most notably at the Museum of Holography in Chicago. Most classes are in the evening and can count toward a college degree.

By completing a core curriculum (cost: around two thousand dollars), you can obtain a diploma in a year or so and be qualified to work as a holographer. This may be the best deal in town, considering full-time, experienced holographers can make around $75,000 a year. However, the equipment (lasers, optical benches) can set you back a few thousand dollars, so you might want to try working for someone else, at least until you're sure this is what you want to do.

Also, this job requires intense levels of concentration, tenacity, and patience. Because it's based on mathematics, absolute precision is necessary. It can be very isolating, so you'd better like the work. But consumers will find your creations brilliant and may regard you as an artistic rocket scientist.

Associations

School of Holography
1134 W. Washington Blvd.
Chicago, IL 60607
312/226-1007

Books

Lasers and Holography. Kock, Winston E. New York: Dover, 1981.

Manual of Practical Holography. Saxby, Graham. Boston: Focal, 1991.

The Making and Evaluation of Holograms. Abramson, Nils. New York: Academic, 1981.

Understanding Holography. Wenyon, Michael. New York: Arco, 1985.

Magazines

Holography
Electronic Imagery
SPIE

Loren Billings
Holographer

Loren Bilings and others at the Museum of Holography in Chicago are spreading the word about their field. "We attract people from all over the world and lecture to school groups. First and second graders go home explaining the physics of light to their parents, and older children are entering holographic exhibits in science fairs."

Although the work requires "total dedication of your time and thoughts," it's quite varied. "Our research and development affiliate deals with an international clientele who utilize holograms on bus passes, in trade shows, and for postage stamps."

In the near future, she believes, holograms will be employed to film movies and television shows, à la the Princess Leia image in *Star Wars*. And we can throw away those 3-D glasses for good.

Photo Researcher

Those who are disorganized and have a tendency to lose things might want to try another field. Photo researchers must pinpoint the images that exactly suit the needs of their clients. When, for example, someone calls you up saying they want a farm scene, you need to ask: Is it vertical or horizontal? Does it include livestock? What about people or buildings? You need to get the picture before sending them the picture.

Ad agencies, graphic design companies, PR departments of corporations, and publishing concerns utilize the services of stock, or generic, photo companies. Using the photo companies is cheaper and less time-consuming than hiring a photographer, although the stock company pays their supplier a percentage (usually half) of the fee they collect. Photographers add to their income by sending photos to the stock companies on consignment.

With hundreds of thousands of images on file, the photo researcher must be able to immediately locate what she's looking for. Pictures are arranged by category, but even finding these requires a keen sense of organization. Let's say you have a picture of senior citizens in a sailboat race. Do you file it under senior citizens, sailing, or competitive sports? (The answer: all three, with a cross-reference in the two files that don't have the photo.)

Losing or incorrectly cataloging a photo can be a disaster. The missing photo could be a thousand places and might never turn up, despite the fact that nothing else will fit the requirements of this particular client.

Most photo researchers have a background in art history or photography and need an excellent memory and eye for detail. Although pay usually starts in the mid-teens, little formal training is required, and many companies operate on a commission in addition to a base salary. Experienced researchers can make around $30,000 per year. Those who own their own companies earn more, but they must also acquire hundreds of thousands of photos and then categorize them. Photographers/rights owners must be notified, and when a photo is sold, permission must be obtained.

Because they deal with so many photos and different clients, researchers must keep impeccable records. These include permission from the photographer and how, where, and by whom the material is to be used.

Associations

American Society of Picture Professionals
c/o H. Armstrong Roberts, Inc.
4203 Locust Street
Philadelphia, PA 19104
(no phone)

Picture Agency Council of America
P.O. Box 308
Northfield, MN 55057
800-457-7222

Books

Stock Photo Deskbook. Persky, Robert, ed. New York: Photographic Arts Center, 1992.
Stock Photography. Purcell, Ann and Carl. Cincinnati: Writer's Digest, 1993.

Magazines

Impressions
International Imaging Sourcebook
Photo Selection
Photo Market
Photobulletin
Daily Photoletter

Mary Ann Platts
Owner, Third Coast

Located in Milwaukee, Wisconsin, Third Coast sends stock photos all over the world. "It doesn't matter where you're based," says owner Mary Ann Platts. "If you've got what customers want, you can get it to them virtually overnight."

Although she's been in business for ten years, "for a long time, I was a one-person band." The company now has a pool of over 300,000 images to offer its more than five thousand customers. Some may need only one photo a year, however, and sometimes none at all.

Currently Platts has four employees and a few part-timers. "But I'm careful about who I hire. They have to be on the same wavelength so everyone here can find images easily. Every stock company has its own unique way of doing things."

Special Occasion Photographer

Most aspiring photographers start small—taking snapshots of friends at weddings, bar mitzvahs, or other special occasions; working part-time or assisting at a shopping mall or a department store; and submitting freelance photos to any publication with a circulation over 250, such as neighborhood newspapers and advertising circulars.

However, those handy with a camera are limited only by their imaginations and can make $5,000 to $10,000 a year working evenings and weekends. Full-timers can earn up to $25,000 or more, but that's a *lot* of pictures. Photo ops abound. Try dance schools, children's sports groups, schools, industries, pet owners, families, and church groups. Aside from two-legged subjects, you can shoot houses and cars (when people invest big bucks, they want to capture their prize for posterity), properties for realtors, crafts and art work for those trying to sell their wares, and products for manufacturers, as well as pictures for advertisers and film stock houses (see Photo Researcher). Most photos involve obtaining written permission from the subjects.

The best advertisements for your work are the pictures themselves: a portfolio of your "greatest hits" shown to potential clients, as well as business cards and fliers to just about anyone who will take them. Start-up costs range from one to five thousand dollars for camera(s) (more than one is often necessary to accommodate a variety of setups), lenses, lights, tripods, backdrops, battery pack, light meters, flashes, and, of course, film, of which there are over a dozen types. The right film can make or break a photo shoot.

Often it's most cost-effective to begin with good used equipment. (State-of-the-art color processing equipment can run into six figures, so it's best left to a lab, which can turn work around quickly and do a great job.) A camera repair shop should inspect all potential purchases beforehand, and employees there are often an excellent source of tips and advice.

Training can be obtained through adult education programs, local community colleges, universities, and even camera stores. After that, just do it.

Associations

American Society of Photographers
P.O. Box 52900
Tulsa, OK 74152
918/743-2122

American Society of Picture Professionals
P.O. Box 5283
Grand Central Station
New York, NY 10063
212/685-3870

National Freelance Photographers Association
10 South Pine Street
Doylestown, PA 18901
215/348-5578

Professional Photographers of America
1090 Executive Way
Des Plaines, IL 60018
312/299-8161

Books

How To Be a Freelance Photographer. Schwarz, Ted. Chicago: Contemporary Books, 1980.
How You Can Make $25,000 a Year With Your Camera. Cribb, Larry. Cincinnati: Writer's Digest Books, 1991.
Photographers' Market. Cincinnati: Writer's Digest Books, updated periodically.
Practical Portrait Photography. Hedgecoe, John. New York: Simon and Schuster, 1988.
The Professional Photographer's Guide to Shooting and Selling. Zuckerman, Jim. Cincinnati: Writer's Digest Books, 1991.

Magazines

American Photographer
Modern Photography
Popular Photography
many others

Julie Smith
Children's Photographer

A mother with three small children, photographer Julie Smith found full-time freelancing burdensome. "Because of my family, working from home was impractical," she says. "I had no place to meet with customers and the phone rang at all hours."

So she signed on with a studio in Worthington, Ohio. "They were looking for a children's photographer and I needed office space and a secretary." Customers call for appointments and Smith works three days a week.

Children are her favorite subjects because they "have no preconceived notions and are very spontaneous." Although her young subjects can present a challenge, "I try to make it fun, to seem like play," she explains. "Kids have very short attention spans, so if I do something unexpected, like hit myself in the head, I get a natural smile."

Videographer

Today anybody can film a video—of their child's birthday party, of a cousin's graduation, even of gaffes that may turn up on local or national TV. But these do not a videographer make. This highly complex, technical field requires courses in television and audio production, including lighting and sound, special effects, editing, camera techniques, script writing, and much more. After that, you can train through interning, working at various production companies, and making your own videos. In the beginning, pay is minimal, if at all.

But after you've proven yourself, there's the wedding, bar mitzvah, and other special occasion circuit; the industrial training, promotional, informational, and advertising route; and if things go really well, actual production of a documentary or fictional drama. You can also make extra money by transferring old home movies to videotape, recording various public events and selling them to interested parties, and doing video "photo albums" of stills for birthdays and anniversaries.

It's best to acquire the basics initially—a video recorder or camcorder, VCR, and good quality microphone. These should run from about one to ten thousand dollars, depending upon whether you rent or purchase. A more complex setup costs a minimum of fifty thousand dollars and includes additional cameras, editing equipment such as sound mixers, digital mixers, and title generators, tripods, lenses, and other extras. But these create more professional results, attracting higher-end clients.

The bread-and-butter jobs of special occasions and individual requests can net from several hundred dollars to the low four figures, depending upon the time and complexity involved. You, the videographer, are present throughout the event and must make sure the final product is cohesive and aesthetically pleasing. Not only does this require an artistic eye, but also an understanding of composition. You must also be both unobtrusive and outgoing, as you may be called upon to thrust a microphone into an unsuspecting drunk's face and ask him to record a few comments about your client's wedding.

More complicated work includes advertisements for companies, public service announcements, industrial training films, even music videos for rock groups. You deal with actors, work on scripts, and scout locations for filming. Before you even shoot the first frame, you might construct a storyboard of various shots, angles, and lighting to be used. Special effects and stunts may also be required.

Such projects demand a great investment of time and require much skill, with payment reaching into the tens of thousands. And who knows? With your profits, you may produce a documentary that wins an Oscar.

Associations

Association of Independent Video and Filmmakers
625 Broadway, 9th Floor
New York, NY 10012
212/473-3400

International Association of Independent Producers
P.O. Box 2801
Washington, DC 20013
202/638-5595

Books

How To Get Started in Video. Cohen, Daniel and Susan. New York: Franklin Watts, 1986

How To Make Your Own Video. Lewis, Roland. New York: Crown, 1987.

John Hedgecoe's Complete Guide to Video. Hedgecoe, John. New York: Sterling, 1992.

Lighting Techniques for Video Production. LeTourneau, Tom. White Plains, NY : Knowledge lndustry, 1986.

Today's Video: Equipment, Setup and Production. Utz, Peter. Englewood Cliffs NJ: Prentice-Hall, 1992.

Magazines

Videography
Videomaker
Videopro
Video Source Book
Video Technology News

Jeremy and Linda Gaynor
Videographers

For years, Jeremy and Linda Gaynor of J & L Productions did "just about anything, even if it didn't pay," says Jeremy. The Coral Springs, Florida, couple worked their way up to weddings and bar mitzvahs and are now focusing on industrial and instructional videos and public service announcements. They always use two cameras for additional footage so nothing is missed.

"We're trying to attract corporate and public agency clients," comments Linda. Current projects include a how-to film on country dancing and a promotional video for a nonprofit organization. The Gaynors also provide special services, such as personalized music videos. "For about $350, you can pick your favorite song and have your friends act out a little play." Needless to say, it's a hit at bar mitzvahs and with teenagers.

"We bend over backward and do extra things for clients, even if it involves working all night," says Jeremy. "We're getting more calls and are starting to get known."

In God we trust. All others pay cash.

—ANONYMOUS

Sales Away

Flea Market Vendor
Home Party Salesperson
Inventor-Seller
Manufacturers' Sales Representative (Pharmaceutical Sales)
Vending Machine Servicer

Flea Market Vendor

In this job, every day is Christmas, as long as you know what you're doing. Flea market vendors can make a tidy profit from other people's junk. By going to garage sales, estate auctions, and through dealings with wholesalers, they find treasures among the trash. Take for a day can range from one hundred to several thousand dollars, if you're at a nationally attended event. But items must be appealing enough to stand out from the gazillions of doohickeys sold by the hundreds of other vendors at the market.

Although little formal training is required to become a vendor, a basic knowledge of retail and a business sense are musts. Those dealing in antiques must know a Chippendale from a Windsor and be able to discern value. They need to study price guides and books and talk with dealers. Vendors of wholesale items need to make sure shipments are delivered on time; what they're selling must also be fairly priced. Customers overpaying on items that fall apart can complain to the manager of the market, and you won't be invited back.

Depending on your location, you may be required to purchase a vendor's license through the state or county and pay sales tax. This involves keeping accurate records. Getting caught without proper documentation can result in a fine or a couple of months in jail for repeated violations.

The other major expense—and it's usually not much—is rent for the booth, which can be about forty dollars a day for an inside setup and half that for an outdoor space. Being indoors allows the advantage of selling in all kinds of weather, but, as a rule, prices are usually higher and traffic slower, especially if it's a nice day. The market center is often the best location, since shoppers aren't yet tired and are not fearful of purchasing too soon.

Most markets are held on weekends, so this job can severely limit family time and social life. Markets may purportedly open at 9:00 A.M. but by 7:00, avid shoppers may be on the prowl for bargains with their flashlights. So you need to be there and set up early. Taking your drive time into consideration, you may have to get up around the same hour as some people who are going to bed and put in a full day's work as well.

A vendor must also be on the lookout for shoplifters. They often work in pairs—one talks to the dealer while the other pockets the goods. Large handbags and big overcoats are usually tipoffs to potential thieves. Even other dealers with large boxes may give your merchandise its walking papers.

Along with having enthusiasm for your wares, you should be outgoing and gregarious, but not so much so that you punch the first person who insults you. Flea market vendors deal with a wide range of buyers, from interior decorators searching for the right touch for their client's million-dollar mansion to questionable characters looking to add to their collection of Nazi memorabilia. Most customers are in between, and if you sell to at least some of them, you'll have big wads of cash and a lighter load to take home.

Associations

Antique Dealers Association of America
Box 632
Newburyport, MA 01950
508/463-4325

Various specialized collectors associations

Books

The Flea Market Handbook. Miner, Robert G. Radnor, PA: Wallace-Homestead, 1990.
The Official Directory of U.S. Flea Markets. New York, NY: House of Collectibles, updated periodically.
Price Guide to Flea Market Treasures. Rinker, Harry L. Radnor, PA: Wallace-Homestead, 1993.
U.S. Flea Market Directory. LaFarge, Albert. New York: Avon, 1993.

Magazines

American Country Collectibles
Classic Amusements
Loose Change
Also official price guides to specific items

Clark and Nancy Potter
Antique Vendors

Clark and Nancy Potter of Lisbon, New Hampshire, scour the countryside during the week in search of antiques, preparing for Saturday and Sunday. "You need a good eye and a working knowledge of the better quality stuff," says Clark. "Otherwise, you might miss something valuable because it looks worn down and cheap."

The Clarks are proficient at refurbishing and repainting. "The more attractive an item is, the likelier you'll catch someone's eye," he adds. "If it has potential, we buy it and fix it up."

Still, "this is hard work. You may lug a piece of merchandise to ten flea markets before you finally sell it—that's packing and unpacking something almost twenty times. And you have to be nice, even to nasty people who try to gyp you." But the majority of dealers and customers "are really delightful. It's like being part of a big extended family."

Home Party Salesperson

This job presents many opportunities for mothers with young children or people who prefer not to work in an office. Direct sales of cosmetics, jewelry, skin care products, cookware, books and encyclopedias, and toys have enabled many women—and a few men—to combine family life with a successful career. You must be willing to work evenings and weekends as well as to open your home to strangers or organize parties at their houses. And your salary will likely be on commission, a percentage of the sales you generate.

You have to keep an eye out for the pitfalls, though. People sometimes make the mistake of going with enterprises that have illegal pyramid schemes or promise great riches in a short period of time (if it sounds too good to be true, it usually is). They may invest a great deal of money to purchase untried inventory, or sign on with a product they're neither excited nor educated about. Because they work from home, they may take a casual approach, failing to follow up on every lead and becoming discouraged by prospect turndowns. As with any other job, you're expected to work hard, adhere to company policies, and always be professional.

But those who stick with solid establishments such as Mary Kay cosmetics, Tupperware, or World Book Encyclopedia, can work as little or as much as they like, using their selling as a sole source or supplemental income.

Home party sellers must have excellent speaking skills; presenting the product to potential customers is all-important. They need to give compelling reasons why purchasers shouldn't go out and buy something similar at the store. They provide product education and historical background and offer incentives so that others will host parties for *their* friends. Combine these with peer pressure, and you've got powerful inducements to buy.

Most sales are in the home, through a combination of one-on-one and party plan selling. Start-up costs are minimal; you don't even need to go out and buy new clothes. Your "office" can be the kitchen table, and although there are no royalty or franchise fees, you will be receiving products and training from the company. You will also be in regular contact with a district manager or supervisor who provides support and guidance.

You can have nine kids or be eighty-five years old; as long as you produce, you'll continue to have a job. And there are few greater incentives and confidence builders than getting paid for work you did on your own initiative—without a boss and a bureaucracy to back you up.

Associations

American Marketing Association
250 S. Wacker
Chicago, IL 60606
312/648-0536

Direct Selling Association
1776 K Street NW
Washington, DC 20006
202/293-5760

Sales and Marketing Management International
Statler Office Tower, No. 458
Cleveland, OH 44115
216/771-6650

Books

Be Your Own Sales Manager. Alessandra, Anthony. New York: Prentice-Hall, 1990.

The Direct Marketing Handbook. Nash, Edward L. New York: McGraw-Hill, 1992.

Direct Sales. Ross, Joyce M. Gretna, LA: Pelican, 1991.

How To Sell Yourself. Girard, Joe. New York: Warner, 1979.

Opportunities in Sales Careers. Dahm, Roger and James Brescoll. Lincolnwood, IL: NTC, 1988.

Personal Selling. Marks, Ronald B. Boston: Allyn and Bacon, 1991

Personality Selling. Anastasi, Thomas E. New York: Sterling, 1992.

Magazines

Opportunity Magazine
Professional Selling
Sales Manager's Bulletin
Selling Direct
Personal Selling Power

Elaine Swaintek
Longaberger Salesperson and Manager

Elaine Swaintek of Alburtis, Pennsylvania, started with Longaberger over ten years ago, when her children were quite young. "I had no idea this would turn into a full-fledged career," she says. She was given a totally new territory, developing it into one of the company's highest-grossing regions and supervising a sales force of six hundred. Longaberger, a multimillion dollar enterprise, creates pottery, dinnerware, and handcrafted baskets.

Nearly all of the twenty-seven thousand Longaberger sales "consultants" are female. "This company has done a lot for women and emphasizes training and recognition. They have a wonderful product and are family-oriented and ethical."

Swaintek works long hours in a barn on her property, employing a secretary whose child plays with her youngest while the two women make phone calls and do paperwork. "We flex our hours according to the kids' schedules. And if my (consultants) can't find day care for our meetings, we make on-site arrangements."

Inventor-Seller

The first impulse of an inventor, whether of a better pooper-scooper or a cure-all diaper-rash cream, is to patent his miracle. The second is to approach a big manufacturer and expect a payoff of millions for retirement to Tahiti.

It's time for a reality check. Most inventions are ignored by the corporate empire. With so many layers of bureaucracy, it's virtually impossible to get to the key decision-maker, if there is one at all (he or she may also have to answer to a board of directors, CEO, and several levels of vice-presidents).

So, as an inventor, you may end up marketing the product or service yourself. Which is not such a bad idea, as long as you do your homework—attend small business and entrepreneurship seminars at the local community college or high school, research costs and manufacturing requirements, study the available market, and compile a business plan. The library is an immense—and free—source of information.

The first question to ask before unleashing your invention on the world is: Will enough people fork over their hard-earned cash to support the enterprise? Is there really a *need* for this diaper-rash cream? Test-marketing the item is one way to find out; approach the stores and offer to sell the product on consignment. Make sure it's displayed prominently; shops are often more likely to promote homegrown innovations. Ads in newspapers and magazines may also stimulate orders by mail. If your invention proves successful, you may have something (be sure to have enough inventory on hand to promptly fill orders). There's no nicer feeling than getting money for your brainchild.

You can also approach a university or research group to do comparison tests (see Product Tester) and thus prove your commodity's effectiveness against competitors. This is a great selling tool. But be warned: Advertising can be expensive. A fair, such as the American Toy Fair, or an exhibition for people in your or related industries, is a smart way to get exposure and meet potential clients.

Also consider legal requirements. Will your invention need FDA approval? What are the components of competitors' products? If you accidentally duplicate their name or commodity, you could be liable. Because you must patent your invention and protect its copyright, it might be wise to consult a lawyer.

In order to underwrite a full-blown enterprise, you may need a bank loan. This is best accomplished by showing the loan officer records and receipts of sales as well as orders for the future. The bank will do a thorough background and credit check.

Franchises and a sales force may be an eventuality, but a too-quick expansion is often the death knell for many small businesses. So be your own salesperson, secretary, and CEO, at least for a while.

Associations

Affiliated Inventors Foundation
2132 E. Bijou Street
Colorado Springs, CO 80908-5950
719/635-1234

American Society of Inventors
P.O. Box 58426
Philadelphia, PA 19102
215/546-6601

Inventors Clubs of America
P.O. Box 450261
Atlanta, GA 30345
404/938-5089

Inventors Guild
Box 132
Plainview, TX 79073
(no phone)

National Inventors Foundation
345 W. Cyprus Street
Glendale, CA 91204
818/246-6540

Books

The Complete Handbook of Profitable Trade Show Exhibiting. Christman, Christine. Englewood Cliffs, N.J.: Prentice-Hall, 1991.

Getting Business To Come to You. Edwards, Paul. Los Angeles: J. P. Tarcher, 1991.

Growing Your Home Business. Gordon, Kim T. Englewood Cliffs, N.J.: Prentice-Hall, 1992.

Handbook for Protecting Ideas and Inventions. Foltz, Ramon D. Cleveland: Penn Institute, 1992.

Patent It Yourself, 3rd ed. Pressman, David. Berkeley, CA: Nolo, 1992.

Magazines

Inventing and Patenting Sourcebook
Invention Intelligence
Inventor's Digest
Inventor's Gazette

Richard Scott
Dog Butler

He doesn't like rainy days and always watches where he walks when on the job, but Richard Scott has the real poop on marketing his own invention, a new and better dog doo cleanup and disposal system. "By necessity, I have to be very careful about what I tell people," observes the owner of the Dog Butler, which is based near Seattle. "There's a lot of competition looking to duplicate salable ideas."

Formerly manager of a grocery store, Scott wanted to find something that hadn't been done before, along with being his own boss (he calls himself an "entremanure"). The removal service, which comes to peoples' homes on a regular basis and rids their yards of Rover's deposits, "had great potential, especially since so many husbands and wives work. Once people found out about us, they even purchased a second dog."

Although his overhead isn't much (scooping devices, biodegradable plastic bags), the problem of dumping the waste must be addressed. "It has to be handled properly and cleared by state and county authorities." In that respect, he's totally clean.

Manufacturers' Sales Representative (Pharmaceutical Sales)

Given today's dicey health care climate, why would anyone want to become a pharmaceutical sales representative (PSR)? A few answers: Salaries *start* at around $35,000 (with the average being $50,000 to $60,000); there will always be a need for prescription drugs; PSRs get to travel to meetings, training sessions, and other gatherings at exciting, major locales; whenever a new product is launched, the company spares no expense in its promotion; you get to be around medical professionals without the attendant gore. And, if for some reason you don't like the job, the skills you acquire can be transferred to another manufacturers' rep position.

Manufacturers' reps have the advantages of choosing the product they want to sell, be it computer chips or designer clothes; being their own boss (within certain parameters); controlling their earning power and job security; working from home and selecting their own hours (again, within reason), and having business expenses (such as car, travel, and client meals) paid for. In return, you provide enthusiasm and in-depth knowledge about the company's product, are self-motivated and well-organized, have excellent communications skills, and serve as a first-line representative of the company by dressing and acting appropriately. So you may have to trade the Walkman, jeans, and army boots for a dark suit and laptop.

PSRs must be able to condense a complex idea into a two-to-three-minute presentation for a busy doctor or medical student who really doesn't want to listen in the first place. This requires patience, persistence, and tact as well as comprehension of drug interactions, side effects, and competing medications. The company equips you with information packets as well as with samples of the drug (the latter must be accounted for).

Although a college degree (preferably in science or business) is required to be a PSR, it is not necessary for all manufacturers' reps. But breaking in can be difficult without previous sales experience or training in a product-related field. Still, most companies offer intensive in-house instruction that can range from a few weeks to, in rare cases, a couple of years. PSRs go through about four months of classroom and on-the-job training. They are also periodically given updates and given "refresher" courses as developments occur in the industry.

Pharmaceutical sales is a highly competitive field, both inside and out. You are selling information, rather than taking orders for a product, and the figures are reflected by the amount of prescriptions filled for the item in your territory. As with many other disciplines, your rivals may have similar products, so you must come up with inventive (but legal) ways to make it especially appealing, or give specific reasons why yours stands out.

People might think sitting around in doctors' offices with a sample case looks easy. But as anyone who's ever sold anything professionally knows, there's no such thing as a free lunch, even if your company is paying for it.

Associations

American Council on Pharmaceutical Education
311 W. Superior Street, Suite 512
Chicago, IL 60610
312/664-3575

American Society for Clinical Pharmacology and Therapeutics
1718 Gallagher Road
Norristown, PA 19401
610/825-3838

Drug Chemical and Allied Trades Association
2 Roosevelt Ave., Suite 301
Syosset, NY 11791
516/496-3317

Pharmaceutical Manufacturers Association
110 15th Street, NW
Washington, DC 20005
202/835-3400

Books

Earning What You're Worth? Dudley, George M. Dallas: Behavior Science Research, 1992.
Key Account Selling. Hanan, Mack. New York: Anacom, 1993.
Successful Large Account Management. Miller, Robert B., et al. New York: Holt, 1991.
Your Home Office. Schreiber, Norm. New York: Harper & Row, 1990.

Magazines

Archives of Internal Medicine
Journal of the American Medical Association
New England Journal of Medicine
Resident & Staff Physician

Scott Hedrick, Pharmaceutical Sales Representative

"This is a very conservative industry," observes Scott Hedrick, who works for a major pharmaceutical company. "It's important to maintain a white collar, professional image."

The Powell, Ohio–based rep finds himself putting in more hours than simply nine to five. He works on weekends and in the evenings, if the situation demands it. "Along with maintaining and prospecting new clients and developing relationships with hospitals and pharmacies, you must be able to find information quickly and sift through astronomical amounts of paperwork. Doctors ask lots of questions and you need to give concise and accurate answers."

Despite the fact that pharmaceutical companies face an uncertain future, those with ambition can succeed in this field. "I trained with former medical students, school teachers, even a store owner and an opera singer. Companies are looking for strong interpersonal and organizational skills rather than just a degree."

Vending Machine Servicer

Like death and taxes, vending machines are here to stay. You can make money off these dieter's downfalls by either working as a route person for a vending company or purchasing your own machines. For the former, you must be bondable with a valid driver's license, or a special license if you drive a truck. With thousands of dollars of merchandise and cash at your disposal, you will also need to be drug-free and have a clean police record. You may have to wear the company uniform and are expected to look neat at all times.

Vending machine servicers collect coins from change boxes, restock merchandise, update labels to indicate new selections, and adjust temperature gauges. Through a computer or written records, they track the amount of food and drink sold. They clean the machines, making sure that refrigerating and heating units work properly and that the bells and whistles—chutes, change makers, plungers, etc.—are in order. When preventive maintenance fails, they call in the National Guard of the vending machine world—the repairers.

Those who are self-employed must not only know the proper state and local food handling and public health procedures but may need a special food handler's permit or license, depending upon regulations. They are responsible for the purchasing and sanitation of the food, as well as for the proper placement, upkeep, and repair of machines. Income can range from a few hundred to a couple of thousand dollars a month, depending upon the type and number of machines. However, you must deal with vandals, spoilage, and breakdowns, all of which can occur at any hour of the day or night.

This is primarily a man's job, mostly because of the heavy lifting required. The proliferation of soda pop machines has resulted in the transport of hundreds of pounds of cans to various vending areas. Many a servicer has injured his back while hoisting the cans or has slipped and fallen on ice while ferrying them from the truck.

Although a high school diploma is preferred, other qualifications, such as courses in electronics and machine repair may help. Certain vocational programs and technical schools even offer basic electronics programs in vending machines and focus on more advanced devices that utilize microchips in pricing, inventory control, and display. Companies also have their own inhouse training and apprenticeship programs, which can range from six months to three years.

Pay varies from $5 to $14 an hour, with the average being $8 to $10. Union members and those working for large corporations receive higher salaries and the self-employed can make even more. And after a while, you may even find you're no longer tempted by packaged snacks.

Associations

National Automatic Merchandising Association
20 N. Wacker Drive
Chicago, IL 60606-3102
312/346-0370

National Bulk Vendors Association
200 N. LaSalle Street, Room 2100
Chicago, IL 60601
312/346-3100

Books

Bulk Vending Machines: Your Route to Success. McNicolas, Dick. Portland, OR: Publisher's, 1985

Contract Foodservice/Vending. Gardner, Jerry. Boston: Cahners, 1973.

Magazines

American Automatic Merchandiser
Automatic Merchandiser
Vending Machines (Coin Operated)
Star Tech Journal
Vending Times

Roger Summers
Vending Route Driver

Roger Summers of Kansas City, Missouri, has been with the Canteen company for thirty-six years, servicing vending machines in office buildings. "I like being out and about and seeing other people's working conditions," he says. "You get to know them, often as well as your own coworkers."

Much of the job, he believes, consists of good public relations. People may come up to you and make comments or complain about the machines, "so you need to have a positive attitude. It's important to be even-tempered."

Flexibility is also a must. "We're trained to handle a lot of machines, and go to a variety of places. One guy can work in a large plant all day, while another may have four or five different accounts."

> Social tact is making your company feel at home, even though you wish they were.
>
> —ANONYMOUS

Service With a Smile

Chauffeur
Closet Organizer
House Cleaner
Image Consultant
Manicurist/Nail Technician
Nanny
Party Planner

Chauffeur

It may look like "the good life," motoring around town in a stretch limo wearing a tuxedo or sharp-looking uniform, ferrying dignitaries, movie stars, and the rich to various destinations, but being a chauffeur is not all luxury. It requires detailed knowledge of the city in which you're based; upkeep and repair of a vehicle so it looks impeccable and runs smoothly, and tact and patience in dealing with rude customers and heavy traffic.

You are supposed to pick up and deliver people on time and know the location of the major office buildings, hotels, movie theaters, malls, night clubs, restaurants, and other highlights. You assist passengers; opening doors, carrying packages, sheltering them from the rain. They're paying big bucks, so they expect the best; whether it's a group of teenagers going to the senior prom or the Queen of England and her entourage. Thus, the limo's TV, telephone, and other accoutrements must be in working order.

This job also involves a fair amount of training. All limo and van drivers must have a chauffeur's or "hacker's" license, in addition to completing courses on local geography, motor vehicle laws, and safety, as well as on regulations governing their profession. A recent addition in some areas is an English comprehension test; those not passing must take an English class sponsored by the municipality.

Certain companies even require training in CPR should something happen to the passenger while in the vehicle. And before they go out on their own, drivers make "test runs" with experienced chauffeurs and managers.

Those going into business for themselves may experience a high rate of failure. Car breakdown, maintenance, costly payments, lack of communication with customers (depending on an answering machine instead of a full-time secretary), insurance, and city licensing expenses can eat up profits. Some localities are governed by specific regulations that make it extremely complicated to operate an independent service. However, business and accounting knowledge as well as mechanical expertise can help reduce expenses.

Most chauffeurs working full-time for a company can make $30,000 to $50,000 a year, including tips, while part-timers earn about $200 a week or more, depending upon how often they're called. Others may be employed by an individual or company that pays their salary; although they may drive fewer hours, they are on call twenty-four hours a day, seven days a week.

Associations

International Brotherhood of Teamsters 1991
25 Louisiana Ave., NW
Washington, DC 20001
202/624-6800
(formerly Chauffeurs, Stableman, and Helpers of America)

International Taxicab and Livery Association
3849 Farragut Ave.
Kensington, MD 20895
310/946-5701

Executive Chauffeuring School
1198 Pacific Coast Hwy., Suite D-232
Seal Beach, CA 90740
310/595-4006

Books

Chauffeur. Syosset, NY: National Learning Corp., 1985.
see also Driver's License Tester and Driving Instructor

Magazines

Limousine and Chauffeur
See also Driver's License Tester and Driving Instructor

John Johnson, Jr.
Limousine Service Owner

In the competitive Houston market, John Johnson, Jr., is glad to be part of Carey Limousine, a national franchise. "We have a certain clientele that uses us whenever they travel," he says. "They know what to expect from us and we, in turn, have a good rapport with them." Of the dozens of limousine services listed in the phone book, "maybe 50 percent of them will last a year."

Johnson's drivers have chauffeured notables from Lassie to Tom Hanks to members of the Republican national convention. "No matter who it is, we never discuss our clients."

Chauffeurs are expected to be personable and know alternative routes in case of traffic problems. "They must be able to communicate well and clearly explain how to get to destinations" once passengers are on their own. "People think this is easy money, but it's hard work."

Closet Organizer

In today's conservative economy, more people are making do with what they have, rather than moving it to a larger home. This is good news for the closet organizer, who specializes in making an immense amount of stuff fit neatly and logically into a small space. Human beings have a tendency to be pack rats, especially if the clutter can be kept in some semblance of order.

Closet organizers go into a residence, measure spaces, and create a design that fits the customer's needs. They suggest what to throw out and explain how to organize similar items and plan for their easy retrieval. They may draw up diagrams, or blueprints, which illustrate where hats, coats, shoes, and other items will be placed. Each type of storage space has specific requirements. For instance, a young child's closet needs more shelves for toys and games and smaller dimensions for clothes and shoes. This type of planning can be done for the entire house, from the kitchen to the bathroom to the garage. Even storage spaces in vehicles and yachts can be whipped into shape.

Closet organizers also need a flair for the ingenious so they can provide a touch of color or sense of uniqueness to the overall design. Customers want to feel they're getting a wide array of options—wire baskets and shelving, stacked shelves, shoe tiers, slide-out drawers, garment bags, cubbyholes (or cubbies), racks, bins and other special items that help to personalize space and make the most chaotic life easier.

Although the job doesn't require much formal training, a background in design or retail is helpful. Spatial and mathematical ability, attention to detail, and tact and good listening skills are necessary. Many times a customer has a specific idea in mind, and you, the closet organizer, need to clearly explain why it will or will not work without offending him or her. There must also be a mutual understanding about exactly what is needed and what is to be done. In this business, clients are like the Holiday Inn—they don't want surprises.

During the initial consultation, you'll have to think quickly and be observant, making suggestions customers can immediately recognize as helpful and tailored to their needs. Although they may not immediately agree to the service, or else decide to use it only for a very small area, they may be back later, once they realize the benefits of locating things easily.

Pay averages about $10 to $15 an hour; more in large cities or for well-known organizers. Most customers are charged by the linear foot; you may also sell them supplies and make a commission on those.

For the closet organizer, recidivism is the name of the game. No matter how large or little the house or space, *something* always needs to be put in order.

Associations

National Association of Professional Organizers
655 N. Alvernon, Suite 108
Tucson, AZ 85711
602/322-9753

Books

Closets. Coen, Patricia and Bryan Milford. New York: Weidenfeld and Nicolson, 1988.

Organized Closets and Storage. Culp, Stephanie. Cincinnati: Writer's Digest Books, 1990.

It's Here . . . Somewhere. Fulton, Alice and Pauline Hatch. Cincinnati: Writer's Digest, 1986.

Shelves, Closets, and Cabinets. Jones, Peter. New York: Popular Science, 1987.

Magazines

Organizing News

Rick Lovelady
Closet Organizer/Retailer

Rick Lovelady of Let's Get Organized sees his job as encompassing both retail and interior design. Along with providing consultation, his Birmingham, Alabama, employer also sells storage supplies. "When people walk in the door for the first time, they're not sure of what they want," he says. "I'm here to help them get control of whatever space they have in mind."

Lovelady's experience helps him cross-reference uses for items. "After you've heard one hundred descriptions of the same problem, you immediately recognize what customers are after. They also appreciate it when you come up with an imaginative use for a shelf or basket" that may not be apparent from its original design.

"We want people to leave happier than when they came in," he says. "Feeling organized helps you feel better."

House Cleaner

Three things are certain: death, taxes, and dirt. Those who prefer not to deal with the latter can hire a cleaning or maid service. Consisting of groups of two or more, these services have replaced the loyal family retainers who used to come in several times a week while the lady of the house went shopping or to the beauty parlor. Now they charge five times as much, stay a few hours, and are usually gone by the time the woman gets home from her full-time job to cook dinner. Is this progress, or what?

Cleaning services are preferred over individuals because they usually bond their employees, which provides a sense of security while the homeowner is out. They also tend to be reliable; if the regular cleaner becomes ill or is called out of town, a substitute can be provided.

So it's best to start out with a reputable company with the goal of eventually establishing your own service. Or you can work part-time to supplement your income. You're getting money for what you're expected to do for free at home and can work independently, without the constraints of an office setting.

Few formal skills are required, except cleaners do need an eye for detail and should be good with their hands. They must also have an idea of exactly what should be tidied up in the time allotted. You don't want to spend four hours scrubbing grout in a bathroom with a toothbrush. Cleaners should be in good physical condition with spotless police and credit records.

You can bring your own supplies or have the client provide them. The latter enables you to cut costs and charge less, but you run the risk of arriving at the home and not having what you need. A good compromise might be to have backup materials in your car and add an equitable charge if they're used.

Some contracts call for occasional or heavy-duty service, focusing on walls, floors, and appliances. Others are on a weekly or bi-weekly basis, consisting of more routine vacuuming, dusting, and bed-changing. Customers are charged less for regular jobs because they're not as difficult, while the service is guaranteed a steady income.

Most training is done on the job, under the supervision of an experienced cleaner. Pay ranges from minimum wage to around $10 an hour. The more proficient and in demand you become, the more the take. However, those with sweeping notions about cleaning up financially usually go elsewhere; turnover in these jobs is fairly high.

Perhaps most important, you need to be customer-service oriented and want to please people. There's lots of competition out there and nothing dishes out dirt faster than bad word of mouth.

Associations

Cleaning Management Institute
13 Century Hill Drive
Latham, NY 12110-2197
518/783-1281

National Executive Housekeepers Association
1001 Eastwind Drive, Suite 301
Westerville, OH 43081-3361
614/895-7166

Books

Cleaning Up for a Living. Aslett, Don and Mary Browning. White Hall, VA: Betterway, 1991.

Dirt Busters. Dasso, Margaret. Lafayette, CA: Peters and Thorton, 1991.

Everything You Need To Know To Start a House Cleaning Service. Johnson, Mary. Seattle, WA: Cleaning Consultant Services, 1979.

Housecleaning Made Easy. Dunne, Margaret. New York: Berkley, 1992.

Managing Housekeeping and Custodial Operations. Feldman, Edwin B. Englewood, Cliffs, NJ: Prentice-Hall, 1992.

Speed Cleaning. Campbell, Jeff. New York: Dell, 1991.

Magazines

Cleaners
Cleaning and Maintenance Management
Pro Principal

Craig Morrison
Cleaning Service Owner

Craig Morrison, owner of the St. Louis–based Mighty Maids, has been in business only a few years. "Initially, there's not much money in this, between overhead, salaries, and turnover," he says. "You also need to be competitively priced."

Still, Morrison enjoys the challenge. "We show new employees a film on how to clean professionally and put them through a thirty-day evaluation period." In addition, they are given an exam.

Cleaners are organized in teams of two so they can keep each other company and boost each other's morale. "A lot of the ladies are homemakers who want to work part-time, recent high school graduates who haven't yet found a job, and single mothers looking for flexible hours."

Morrison feels the field is undervalued and is constantly searching for dependable employees. "It's hard work, but if you can do it well, you'll always have a job."

Image Consultant

To do this job, you must look the part. Image consultants are exquisitely clothed, made up, and coiffed. In fact, they are so impeccable they often stand out from the rest of us—walking advertisements of their best work.

They are also faced with the not-so-pleasant task of gently informing clients—men and women—that among other things, they have bad breath, body odor, and a wardrobe that's wrong for them. But the client may have come to them in tears, sent by spouse, lover, boss, or an employment agency. They need help, and the image consultant is supposed to "fix" the problem, at least externally.

The job involves a knowledge of color analysis (certain hues look better with particular shades of skin and hair), aesthetics (makeup and skin care), even fashion design. Consultants, usually working with a professional stylist, need to be able to recommend makeup, hair style, and clothes that will emphasize the client's best points. They go shopping with clients, helping them pick out and accessorize an entire wardrobe. This is done to accent figure strengths and downplay flaws, rather than to choose the latest fashion or to satisfy the taste of the consultant.

Image consulting can even be carried over into selecting eyeglass frames, home and office decor, and automobiles—anything that will contribute to the total impact of the individual. Consultants also work to improve self-confidence, making suggestions as to effective body language in the office and social world and providing advice on ways to better organize clients' lives and personal effects (see Closet Organizer).

Consultants also work with corporations. Banks, medical groups, insurance companies, and others hire them to provide tips to employees about skin care and wardrobe so that the company will enhance *its* overall image. Teaching is usually done in a classroom setting without the intense one-to-one emphasis.

Pay varies greatly, from $75 to $100 an hour for high-level consultants to $25 an hour for those starting out. How much you can charge depends greatly on your training and experience—courses in color analysis, aesthetics, and other aspects are available at cosmetology and vocational schools and community colleges. Customers will expect you to be up on the latest trends and developments. Even the most well-versed consultants regularly attend seminars and classes.

Although this job deals with the superficial, it requires a great deal of empathy for and understanding of your fellow man and woman. Consultants need creativity, tact, patience, and an outgoing personality. And the color blind should consider another field.

Associations

Aestheticians International Association
4447 McKinney Ave.
Dallas, TX 75205
800/285-5277

Association of Image Consultants, International
1000 Connecticut Ave., NW, Suite 9
Washington, DC 20036
800/383-8831

Institute of Personal Image Consultants
10 Bay Street Landing, Suite 7F
Staten Island, NY 10301
718/273-3229

Books

Always in Style. Pooser, Doris. Los Altos, CA: Crisp, 1989.
Beautiful Again. Willis, Jan. Santa Fe: Health, 1994.
Beauty Basics. Sesdelli, Maryellen, et al. New York: Berkley, 1993.
Color Me a Season. Kentner, Bernice. Antioch: CA: Kenkra, 1991.
Doing It Right. Laladula, Dorothy. New York: Shapolsky, 1990.
Finishing Touches. Oliver, Anne. New York: Bantam, 1990.
The Good Look Book. Elson, Melvin, et al. Atlanta: Longstreet, 1992

Magazines

Aesthetics World Today
Applied Esthetiques
The Rose Sheet
Real Beauty

Arlene Voepel
Image Consultant

Arlenne Voepel of Phoenix, Arizona, started out doing color analysis for figure skaters. "I was a coach and discovered it greatly improved the appearance of my athletes." She eventually consulted for the U.S. Olympic figure skating team.

Now the owner of Total Image, Voepel has taken intensive training in color analysis and has her esthetician's license. The latter involves courses in facial bone structure, types of skin, massage, makeup, and related subjects. "You need to back up your recommendations with knowledge," she observes. "If you make a mistake, everything has to be thrown out. It hurts both you and the client."

She works with both individuals and corporations. "When clients go out the door smiling or when I get letters saying how my suggestions changed their lives, I forget that I even get paid for this." Until the mortgage comes due.

Manicurist/Nail Technician

Nail technology has come a long way since the days of water manicures at Madge's beauty salon. Today, technicians are expected to be competent in hot oil manicures, pedicures, paraffin therapy, hand and arm massage, and nail sculpting and decoration. The latter is an extremely elaborate craft requiring artistic ability and steady hands. Some customers want rhinestones glued on their nails or may request that each nail have a different tableau. This is serious—and profitable—stuff and the industry is growing as fast as, well, nails.

Through several hundred hours of training at a certified school of cosmetology (see below for associations listing reputable ones), technicians also learn how to apply artificial nails and tips. The many techniques utilize ultraviolet light, silk or linen wraps, fiberglass, acrylics, porcelain, gels, and combinations of liquid and powder. Students must be familiar with dozens of different manufacturers, each of which employs a unique method. They must also be versed in how to open and manage a salon as well as in the state laws that regulate their work. Many schools provide "practice runs," offering the public manicures from students at a reduced cost as well as outplacement services.

All states require barbers and cosmetologists (and thus, usually, nail technicians) to be licensed. This involves graduation from a state-approved cosmetology school and passing a written and demonstration examination as well as a physical. The minimum age requirement is sixteen. Classes may run from a few weeks to several months, depending upon whether you want to study full or part-time. Instruction at vocational schools is also available, as are apprenticeships. Fees can range from fifteen hundred to four thousand dollars.

Although nail technicians can make $50,000 and more annually, including tips, this job is not without hazards. Exposure to dust and chemicals occurs on a regular basis and may result in lung and skin diseases and irritation. Job-related injuries may include carpal tunnel syndrome and eye damage from flying debris. Because they trim cuticles, which can draw blood, technicians may also run the risk of coming into contact with the AIDs virus. Masks, safety glasses, and gloves help circumvent such perils, and may soon become mandatory.

Although schools and employers may provide partial manicure kits, new graduates may need to spend several hundred dollars on drills, a table, and supplies. Those striking out on their own incur the additional expenses involved in running a small business.

Along with manual dexterity and a sense of form and artistry, you'll need to get along with the public, be a good listener, and be willing to follow patrons' instructions. The field is constantly evolving and improving, so trade shows and continuing education classes add to marketability. Then, you may have the whole world at your fingertips.

Associations

Association of Accredited Cosmetology Schools
5201 Leesburg Pike
Falls Church, VA 22041
703/845-1333

Nails Industry Association
2512 Artisia Blvd.
Redondo Beach, CA 90278
800/84-NAILS

Nails Manufacturing Council
401 N. Michigan Ave.
Chicago, IL 60611
312/644-6610

National Accrediting Commission of Cosmetology Arts and Sciences
901 N. Stuart Street, Suite 900
Arlington, VA 22203
703/525-7600

World International Nail and Beauty Association
1221 N. Lakeview
Anaheim, CA 92807
714/779-9883

Books

The Art and Science of Manicuring. Cimaglia, Alice. Bronx, NY: Milady, 1986.

Finger Tips. Ferri, Elisa. New York: C. N. Potter, 1988.

Milady's Guide to Owning and Operating a Nail Salon. Wiggins, Joanne. Albany, NY: Milady, 1994.

Nail Art and Design. Bigan, Tammy. Albany, NY: Milady, 1994.

West's Textbook of Manicuring. Ahern, Jerry. St. Paul: West, 1986.

Magazines

American Salon
Beauty Trends
Gloss
Manicuring Salons
NAILS
Nailpro
NAAC Washington Update

Dee Dunlop
Nail Technician

A former medical care worker, Dee Dunlop was bored by her profession. "I wanted to do my own nails so I went to school to learn how and found that I loved it," she recalls. Now she owns Body by Design, a Pickerington, Ohio, enterprise that employs several technicians.

Despite the recent improvements in the field, Dunlop claims that "the public is still somewhat suspicious" about diseases and problems with false nails, such as fungus. "There are dangers if (fake) nails are improperly set." She emphasizes health and education, making sure each client knows how to care for her nails. Her male customers have yet to request acrylics, although plenty come in for manicures.

"You must be naturally gifted and able to visualize what the hand should look like." Along with his or her fingers, "each client is different."

Nanny

Underlying the myth of Mary Poppins, the TV sitcom *The Nanny,* and the horror flick *The Hand That Rocks the Cradle* is a specialist who works in a family home, caring for children; nurturing their physical, emotional, and social development in addition to changing diapers and wiping noses. Nannies are quite different from babysitters (no training required), au pairs (who do housework in addition to looking after kids), and nursery nurses and governesses (veddy British). Nannies work full or part-time and live in or out of the family home. They range from ages eighteen to seventy and may even include men. They may also receive formal schooling.

Because of the proliferation of two-income families and the scarcity of decent daycare, nannies can pick and choose their situations. Unfortunately, you don't need certification of any kind to call yourself a nanny, which is why families must screen candidates carefully, checking references and even police and driver's license records. Parents have been known to videotape the nanny on the job, making sure she's not abusing or neglecting their child(ren). Nannies and families must also be wise to the IRS, which is always on the lookout for nonpayment of income taxes and Social Security, even contacting nanny placement agencies for names and addresses.

Nannies need to be cautious as well. Help wanted ads, referrals from friends, and bulletin boards may result in not-so-dependable leads and bad experiences; nanny placement agencies evaluate families as carefully as the families evaluate the nannies. And don't be surprised if the agency takes your fingerprints and does a background check, in addition to requiring a blood and TB test and a statement from your doctor that you're in good health.

Many nannies, particularly younger ones, do attend reputable programs (although life experience counts for a lot in the grandmotherly types). These programs range from six intensive weeks to several months for a certificate from a nanny school or two or four-year's for a degree in childhood behavior from a college. Although they can be pricey (up to five thousand dollars), nanny schools are the most practical, offering field practice and training in child development and psychology, family relations, special needs, nutrition, infant stimulation and safety, and pre-academics and creative play, as well as in CPR. Many schools also place graduates.

Once you hook up with the right family, life can be glorious. Salaries can range from $10,000 to $25,000 a year with free room and board, if that's your preferred situation. Families can provide medical insurance, paid vacations, holidays and sick days, and the use of a car. Since many of the families are well-off or in high profile jobs, you may also get to travel with them and enjoy other perks. For all this, you "work" fifty to sixty hours a week. But those who enjoy children will hardly regard this as back-breaking travail.

For many, this job is a stepping-stone to college, marriage, and the formation of their own families. But it will make the trip a lot more interesting.

Associations

American Council of Nanny Schools
c/o Joy Shelton
Delta College
University Center, MI 48710
517/686-9417

International Nanny Association
125 S. Fourth Street
Norfolk, NB 68701
402/691-9628

National Academy of Nannies (NANI)
1681 S. Dayton Street
Denver, CO 80231
800/222-NANI

Books

The Au Pair and Nanny's Guide to Working Abroad. Griffin, Susan and Legg, Sharon. Cincinnati, OH: Writer's Digest, 1989.
Careers in Child Care. Eberts, Marjorie and Margaret Gisler. Lincolnwood, IL: NTC, 1994.
Live-In Child Care. Binswanger, Barbara and Betsy Ryan. New York: Doubleday, 1986.
Nannies, Au Pairs, Mothers' Helpers—Caregivers. Yeiser, Lin. New York: Vintage, 1987.
Working With Young Children. Herr, Judy. South Holland, IL: Goodheart-Willcox, 1990.

Magazines

Childcare
ActioNews
Child Development
association and school newsletters

Tracy Yetter
Nanny

Tracy Yetter of Littleton, Colorado, found the time, money, and effort invested in nanny school "totally worth it. Not only did they teach me all about children, but they placed me with a family while I was learning. This provided me with the confidence and experience to get the job I wanted."

In the past, Yetter lived with families, but now that she's married, she commutes every day. "When you live in, everything you do is under scrutiny. Not only are you with the family constantly, but you must get along with their relatives and neighbors." Regardless of your situation, "you need to be a good role model and not, for example, be constantly going to singles bars or be hung over. You must also be sensitive to how parents want their children raised" rather than imposing your own will or personal beliefs.

The single greatest qualification for a nanny, Yetter believes, is a love of children. "They will know immediately if you're faking it. Babysitters may be able to fool families for a few hours, but when you're a nanny, there's no getting around kids."

Party Planner

A party is supposed to be fun, except for the person organizing it. Myriads of details must be attended to: arranging centerpieces, writing out place cards, making sure cousin Sunshine, who is a vegetarian, doesn't get the roast beef. For large gatherings, such as weddings and bar mitzvahs, florists, caterers, entertainment, invitations, photographers, and videographers (see appropriate chapters) must be dealt with. There is also usually more than one event, such as a rehearsal dinner or brunch. As a party planner, you can come to the rescue. Your client can relax and observe how his or her hard-earned thousands are being spent.

Party planners take care of all aspects, from offering a selection of invitations, to planning the menu, to insuring the flowers are properly placed, to cleaning up the final mess. During the first consultation, they sit down with potential clients, planning the theme of the party and determining the budget. Planners then offer suggestions about the type of entertainment, decorations, place settings, etc. If the cake baker comes down with the flu and can't deliver, it's the planner's responsibility to find a replacement. The only thing the client worries about is whether the groom will show up on time or whether the bar mitzvah boy will forget his lines (most of the congregation likely wouldn't notice anyway).

As a party planner, you can provide little extras clients appreciate; for instance, hospitality baskets in hotel rooms with fruit and cheese for out-of-town guests. It doesn't necessarily have to be expensive; "favors" at a baseball-themed celebration can consist of water bottles with team logos. Your biggest helper is a "black book" of entertainers and businesses specializing in the type of event you're planning. By building good relations with these people and giving them jobs, you can receive special services and discounts. Your "pipeline" provides things for your clientele that will be the envy of their friends.

Conventional training in this field is practically nonexistent, although a home study course in bridal consulting is available from the Association of Bridal Consultants (see below). Vocational schools and colleges also supply classes in business, psychology and sociology, and hotel and food service management.

On a personal level, party planners need to be people-oriented, creative, good communicators, and, most importantly, organized. It won't look good if you get to a wedding and forget the bride's "something blue." For your trouble, you reap about 15 percent of the gross cost of the event, in addition to a consultation fee of $25 to $75 an hour, billed for the time spent with the client (but not the hours and mileage involved in chasing down that perfect ceiling decoration).

This job wreaks havoc with evenings and weekends because most event planners, or their designates, are present to make sure things run smoothly. You may find yourself dealing with frayed nerves, second thoughts, and stage fright, but in the end, you will have very likely helped make someone very happy.

Associations

American Society of Wedding Professionals
268 Griggs Ave.
Teaneck, NJ 07666
800/793-3776

Association of Bridal Consultants
200 Chesterford Road
New Milford, CT 06776
203/355-0464

International Special Events Society
8335 Allison Pointe Trail, Suite 100
Indianapolis, IN 46250
317/577-1910

Books

The Art of the Party. Reynolds, Renny. New York: Viking Studio, 1992.

The Best Party Book. Warner, Penny. Deephaven, MN: Meadowbrook, 1992.

Desmond's Guide to Perfect Entertaining. Atholl, Desmond and Cherkinian, Michael. New York: St. Martin's, 1993.

Emily Post on Entertaining. Post, Elizabeth L. New York: HarperPerennial, 1994.

How To Give Successful Parties. Adamson, Nicky and Stephen. New York: Smithmark, 1991.

How To Plan the Perfect Party. Bennett, Gayle. Scarsdale, NY: NewWay, 1992.

Magazines

Party Design Quarterly
Party Planning Services
Party Supplies
Special Events Magazine

Deborah Kuhr and Barb Guthoff, Party Planners

Deborah Kuhr and Barb Guthoff of RSVP Party Planners met while volunteering to organize a charitable function. "We just clicked," says Kuhr. "Now we finish each other's sentences." Their Pickerington, Ohio, enterprise specializes in bar and bat mitzvahs.

"Organizing this type of event can be overwhelming," Kuhr goes on. "It can consist of several functions in one weekend and since it's once in a lifetime, families want everything to be perfect."

The two women work toward making each bar or bat mitzvah unique. "It should reflect the child's personality and interests," says Kuhr. "If his hobby is magic, then we carry that through the entire weekend." They also tell their clients to pretend they have an unlimited budget. "You can do a lot with just a little. The point is to be imaginative and create an experience people will never forget."

Travel is glamorous only in retrospect

—PAUL THEROUX

Travel Mavens

Adventure Trip Organizer
Cruise Ship Worker
Flight Attendant
Railroad Conductor or Engineer
Tour Guide

Adventure Trip Organizer

Hot-air ballooning, kayaking, dog sledding, ice climbing, windsurfing, hang gliding, skydiving, snowmobiling— temporarily or eternally injuring yourself doing one of these things seems so much more *gratifying* than, say, being mowed down by a car or shot while picking up bread at a convenience store. And as an adventure trip organizer, you can earn a living and pick your own on-the-edge thrills.

Of course, the key to any successful adventure excursion is making it as safe as possible while providing maximum exposure to the mountains, ocean, etc. So organizers need a thorough knowledge of every aspect of whatever adventure package they're putting together. This includes proficiency in a particular sport, such as skiing, as well as contacts within the destination community. Fluency in foreign languages (including the hundreds of dialects spoken in the Third World) is immensely helpful, if not necessary. The term for *bread* in one language may mean *you're ugly* in another.

The importance of in-depth experience and subject familiarity can't be emphasized enough. For instance, a trip to the North Pole, along with costing tens of thousands of dollars, might include a voyage on a nuclear-powered Russian icebreaker or flying to Resolute, Canada, then taking a twin-engine plane to two more remote locations, where passengers may wait up to three days for safe weather conditions to spend a few hours on the Pole. Although you may not be present at every excursion, people are truly putting their lives and pocketbooks in your hands.

Because of the diversity of trips, there is no particular training for this job. However, tour management schools (see Tour Guide) and education in a related field, such as botany and zoology if tours focus on flora and fauna, are beneficial. And business, organization, and writing skills are useful. Having lived or traveled extensively in the area also helps.

Like tour guides, adventure trip organizers must deal with a myriad of details—food, lodging, transfers between various modes of travel—and must be sensitive to the needs of their customers. And it is particularly important not to mislead clientele; someone who enjoys the amenities might not be comfortable on bareboat charter with no crew. One unhappy camper can drag down the entire group. And clients should be well-informed of potential dangers at all times, or they might fall off a frozen waterfall or be trampled by a rhinoceros.

Pay for this job is good—successful organizers can pull in $50,000 to $60,000 a year for three months work. Still, the other nine months are devoted to putting together an itinerary, paying liability insurance premiums, and praying that nothing goes wrong.

Associations

Adventure Travel Society
6551 S. Revere Parkway
Englewood, CO 80111
303/649-9016

American Society of Travel Agents
1101 King Street
Alexandria, VA 22314
703/739-2782

International Tour Management Institute
625 Market Street, Suite 1015
San Francisco, CA 94105
415/957-9489

International Guide Academy
Foote Hall, Suite 313
7150 Montview Blvd.
Denver, CO 80220
303/794-3048

Travel Industry Association of America
2 Lafayette Center
1133 21st Street, NW, Suite 800
Washington, DC 20036
202/408-8422

Books

Adventure Travel Abroad. Dickerman, Pat. New York: Holt, 1986.

Adventure Traveling. Hill, T.J. Bedford, MA: Mills and Sanderson, 1986.

The Adventurous Traveler's Guide. Berkeley: Ten Speed, 1984.
The Ultimate Adventure Sourcebook. McMenamin, Paul. Atlanta: Turner, 1992.

Magazines

Adventure Travel North America
Adventure West
Great Expeditions
Sojourns
Specialty Travel Index

Richard Mills
Trip Organizer

Richard Mills of International Expeditions in Helena, Alabama, eased into planning and coordinating treks to Africa and South America. With a master's in zoology and teaching and curatorial experience, he began his career by going into the deepest jungles and extracting vampire bats, salamanders, and other creepy crawlies for various organizations. Everyone, including the specimens, returned alive and well.

Today, however, says Mills, "I organize the trips, writing up detailed itineraries, making sure accommodations are comfortable." Also, "because we focus on natural history and educational content, I make sure the trip is geared toward learning about birds, plants, reptiles, and other mammals.

"We try to build in flexibility for people with differing interests." The best solution, however, is consumer education. "We tell them in advance what to expect."

Cruise Ship Worker

If you're single, love to travel, and are a beautician, massage therapist, entertainer, exercise instructor (see appropriate chapters), or have accounting, casino, medical, or secretarial experience, this may be the perfect job for you. (Room steward, waiter, and maintenance positions are usually taken by foreign nationals, while the ship's officers are trained through their country's marine academy or government.)

Because room and board are paid for, you can save most of your salary, as long as you don't go overboard at the various ports of call. You can travel to exotic places, meet fascinating people, and have a rich social life with all the other single, attractive workers on the ship. However, those with claustrophobia or a dislike of water need not apply.

A cruise ship is a self-contained world. And as a representative of the cruise line, you are constantly "on" for the passengers. You need to smile, or at least look pleasant, at all times, regardless of whether you've got the flu or had a fight with your current flame. And you should truly enjoy meeting new people, because a boatload arrives every week or so. On the other hand, you never get bored with the same faces and have a good excuse if you forget someone's name.

Cruise workers need to be ambitious, eager to please, and outgoing. On smaller ships, particularly, they must be available to pitch in and help wherever necessary; for instance, the purser may also help organize a limbo contest. Even if your job isn't one that involves tips, service is the name of the game.

Cruise lines are constantly expanding and turnover is high—workers grow disenchanted with the lifestyle, get married, or miss their families. So opportunities do arise. The best way to find out about jobs is to contact cruise lines (a few are listed below). Depending upon the job, you may also have to join a maritime union.

Still, working on a cruise ship is a once-in-a-lifetime experience. Granted, you may have to share a tiny cabin with another employee and may miss the latest edition of *Wheel of Fortune* but you will have many tales for your grandchildren.

Associations

Cruise Lines International Association
500 Fifth Ave., Suite 1407
New York, NY 10110
212/921-0066

National Maritime Union
P.O. Box 77520
Washington, DC 20013
202/347-8585

Some major cruise lines:
Carnival Cruises
3655 Northwest 87th Ave.
Miami, FL 33178
800/438-6744

Norwegian Cruise Lines
95 Merrick Way
Coral Gables, FL 33134
800/327-7030

Royal Caribbean
1050 Caribbean Way
Miami, FL 33102
800/443-5789

Books

Guide to Cruise Ship Jobs. Reilly, George. Babylon, NY: Pilot, 1989.

How To Get a Job With a Cruise Line. Miller, Mary F. St. Petersburg, FL: Ticket to Adventure, 1994.

Magazines

Cruise Industry News
Cruise News
Cruise and Freighter Travel Letter

John Heald
Cruise Director

Coordinating over two hundred activities for twenty-six hundred passengers keeps John Heald of Carnival Cruise Lines on the run. "People are spending their hard-earned money and vacation time and expect the best," observes the British-born cruise director, whose background includes stints as an insurance broker and wine steward. "After a few days, they all know who I am." Heald sometimes finds himself peppered with such questions as "What do you with the ice carvings after they've melted?" and "Does this elevator go to the back of the ship?"

The environment of a cruise brings out hidden talents. "I was always a bit of a clown in school, but never did a comedy show until I started working on a ship." And unlike most people, he flees *toward* inclement weather during his vacation. "We work seven days for six months, then get several weeks off," he says. "I like to take my time during the winter, away from water." But he wouldn't have it any other way: "On the ship, you meet some incredibly nice people and see fantastic places."

Flight Attendant

Flight attendants have come a long way from the days when they had to be short (low ceilings on aircraft), slim (less weight on the plane), and young and female (attractive to passengers, mostly male businessmen). They still need to be perky and enthusiastic, and in excellent health, with good vision and hearing. If this sounds suspiciously like the qualifications for a race horse, you've got an idea of the competition this field engenders. For every position opening, there are hundreds, possibly even thousands of applicants.

Although some private schools offer general course work for flight attendants, such classes are not likely to increase your odds of getting a job. New hires receive four to six weeks of training from the airline in emergency procedures (evacuation, operating the oxygen system, first aid), flight regulations and duties, company operations and policies, and personal grooming and weight control. Age or sex doesn't matter these days, but flight attendants must maintain that patina of glamour, poise, and great wisdom about the mysterious workings of an airplane.

Although a high school degree is a basic requirement, more airlines are looking for postsecondary education or equivalent life experience. A background in customer service, hospitality, nursing, or even psychology adds to employability. It also helps to be fluent in one or more foreign languages for international flights. Then, as a bonus, you receive additional training in passport and custom regulations and dealing with terrorism.

After classes, you're assigned a home base, or domicile, at one of the major cities where the airline is located. You may be on reserve for several months, filling in for sick or vacationing attendants. Once off reserve, you can bid for a regular assignment, but the choice routes are usually given to those with the most seniority.

You will be expected to work evenings, weekends and holidays, and may have out-of-town layovers of several days. When on the job, you'll toil long hours—helping store luggage and carry-ons, offering blankets and reading material, serving food and drink, and dealing with questions and complaints. Before each takeoff, you get to explain (or listen to a tape explain) yet again how to fasten the seat belt along with what to do during an emergency. Most people who can't do the former are under age two and won't pay attention anyway.

Along with dealing with illness and administering first aid, attendants must make sure children, the disabled, and the elderly are comfortable. You must remain calm and reassure passengers in the event of turbulence, instructing them in evacuation procedures should the plane have to make an emergency landing.

The job doesn't end there—there are reports on medications administered, lost and found articles, and cabin conditions to prepare. And being late for any flight is a no-no, since attendants are expected to show up for a briefing one hour before scheduled departure.

Over the years, airlines have become more flexible in promoting from within and allowing their attendants to transfer to related jobs, such as instructor, customer service representative, etc. So turnover is not as high as it once was. But if you get hired (at about $13,000 per annum), you'll receive pay increases that may eventually bring you to $40,000 a year, free or discounted travel, health and other benefits, and reimbursement for expenses while on the job. Perhaps the only loftier position is that of a pilot and he (or she) can garner an annual salary of around $150,000.

Associations

Air Line Employees Association
5600 South Central Ave.
Chicago, IL 60638-3797
312/767-3333

Association of Flight Attendants
1625 Massachusetts Ave., NW, #300
Washington, DC 20036
202/328-5400

Air Transport Association of America
1709 New York Ave., NW
Washington, DC 20006
202/626-4000

Future Aviation Professionals of America
4959 Massachusetts Blvd.
Atlanta, GA 30337
800/JET-JOBS

Independent Federation of Flight Attendants
630 Third Ave.
New York, NY 10017
212/818-1130

Books

Careers As a Flight Attendant. Lobus, Catherine O. New York: Rosen, 1991.
The Flight Attendant Career Guide. Kirkwood, Tim. Delray Beach, FL: TKE, 1993.
Guide To Becoming a Flight Attendant. Kinian, Douglas. Holbrook, MA: Bob Adams, 1987.
Opportunities in Travel Careers. Milne, Robert. Lincolnwood, IL: NTC, 1991.
Travel. Miller, Robert. Princeton, NJ: Peterson's, 1993.

Magazines

Airlines
Airliners Monthly News
Airport Press
Air Travel Journal
Airfair
Flying Times

Leo Katigbak
Flight Attendant, MGM Grand Air

As a representative of one of the world's most exclusive and expensive airlines, Los Angeles-based Leo Katigbak has met movie stars, athletes, even the president of the United States. But he can't talk about it: "All MGM Grand Air flight attendants must sign privacy waivers."

This unique airline has scheduled legs between New York, Las Vegas, and Los Angeles as well as charter flights to other destinations. Although it utilizes Boeing 727s, this is hardly steerage: the plane, which normally seats 137 passengers, has individual and stateroom accommodations for only 34. Forget TV-dinner style "airplane food"; cuisine is prepared on board by professional chefs. Meals consist of several courses, hors d'oeuvres, and complimentary drinks. The airline also offers curbside check-in, private lounges, lumbar seats, and other amenities.

The personalized service makes it especially challenging for attendants. "We work harder, because we treat people as if they're guests in our living room," explains Katigbak. He has even braved the language barrier in a foreign city to obtain specific foodstuffs based on passenger requests. "When the airplane stops, your job doesn't. But the payoff comes because you're making people happy."

Railroad Conductor or Engineer

This may be every little boy's (and some girls') dream, but the reality is that the work is hard and unpredictable and that technology and computerization have reduced jobs, particularly entry-level positions such as brake operators (who help conductors) and firemen (assistant engineers). Still, engineers can earn an average of $55,000 a year, while conductors receive a median of $38,000. There are excellent benefits and union protection that provides railroad workers with a semblance of job security, although work can be seasonal.

Along with shouting "All aboard!," conductors working on passenger trains collect tickets and fares and answer questions about operations and timetables. They also signal engineers when to pull out of the station at stops and supervise the overall operation of the train.

The majority of conductors who work on freight trains are also in charge of train and yard crews. They can be either road conductors or yard conductors (should the trucking and railway industries ever combine, perhaps there will be a need for semi conductors). They maintain a written or computerized record for cars, along with insuring their removal and addition at appropriate points along the route. Road conductors travel with the train, obtaining instructions and discussing the itinerary, cargo, and timetable with the engineer before departure. During the run, they are constantly in touch with the engineer and dispatchers at the various stations regarding track conditions, stops, and the presence of other trains.

Yard conductors supervise crews that put together and take apart the trains. Some cars go to certain tracks for unloading, while others are moved to an area for recoupling with other trains destined for different cities. Yard conductors instruct engineers where to move cars and tell brake operators which cars to couple or uncouple and which switches to throw to divert cars or the train to the proper track. Freight conductors spend most of their time outdoors in all kinds of weather and must do heavy physical labor when required.

Engineers have it a bit easier, and although they are expected to know all signal systems, yards, and terminals, their responsibilities lie mostly with the train. They must be constantly aware of how the individual locomotive reacts to acceleration, braking, and curves based on the number of cars, weight of the freight, and the amount of slack between the cars. Like conductors, some engineers operate trains carrying cargo and passengers while others move cars within yards for assembly and disassembly.

The engineer's job requires constant attention. Driving a train is like trying to walk, juggle, and chew gum at the same time. Factors to watch for include brake pressure, speed, fuel level, temperature, battery charge, track conditions, speed limits, and movement of other trains, among others. In addition to extensive railroad experience and a six-month training program, engineers must pass qualifying tests covering every aspect of train operation. They must also submit to regular physical fitness exams to retain their status.

The best entry into these jobs is to start at the lowest level and work your way up. Although seniority will provide regular employment, you can forget about choosing your own hours. Most freight trains are unscheduled, and when your name comes up, it's time to hop on board, even if they blow the whistle at 3 A.M.

Associations

Association of American Railroads
50 F Street, NW
Washington, DC 20001
202/639-2550 or 2190

Order of Railway Conductors and Brakemen
United Transportation Union
14600 Detroit Ave.
Lakewood, OH 44107-4250
216/228-9400

Books

Back on Track. Lowe, Marcia D. Washington, DC: Worldwatch Institute, 1994.

Manual for Railway Engineering. Washington, DC: American Railway Engineering Association, updated periodically.

Opportunities in Travel Careers. Milne, Robert. Lincolnwood, IL: NTC, 1991.

The Railroad. Armstrong, John H. Omaha, NE: Simmons-Boardman, 1990.

Train Talk. Yepsen, Roger. New York: Pantheon, 1983.

Magazines

Coupler
Locomotive Engineers Journal
Passenger Train Journal
Progressive Railroading
Rail News Update

Dave Birckbichler
Freight Engineer

Dave Birckbichler of Columbus, Ohio, has been "workin' on the railroad" since 1973. A former brake operator, he advanced to yard and road conductor, and is now being trained as an engineer.

As a conductor and engineer, "you need to get along with a variety of people. Each run has a different crew, so you must be able to communicate well." Birckbichler is also finding that the jobs require an increasing amount of computer skills for personnel, freight, and car recordkeeping as well as automation on the train itself, which indicates, for instance, various malfunctions.

"As a conductor, I might be out in the elements, changing an eighty-pound knuckle (connector) that uncoupled two cars, or acting as a liaison between various groups if there's an emergency. Although the job sometimes wreaks havoc with my sleeping habits and family, I enjoy the uncertainty."

Tour Guide

What a trip! Tour guides are responsible for a group's hotel, dining, and travel arrangements; entertainment and medical concerns; and information about the destination. This is a twenty-four hours a day, seven days a week job with little or no personal time, and no allowances for either male or female PMS. At worst, it can be akin to herding cats; at best, it's rewarding and exciting because you're paid to go to exciting places, meet interesting people, and you can take long vacations (which you'll need after weeks and months of nonstop travel). Plus, you never have to cook a meal!

But, to become successful, you'll need a lot of experience, and not just formal training, although travel schools and community colleges do offer instruction (tour management programs are listed below). Tour guides must know the customs and geography of every attraction, the language if it's in a foreign country, and they must be conversant with regional flora, fauna, and history, which requires research and study. They also work closely with hotel, reservation, and destination staff to make sure things run smoothly.

On a personal level, you need to be organized, resourceful, in excellent physical condition for long and grueling days of travel, and have good speaking and communications skills. You should also be able to tread the line between tact and assertiveness, a feat requiring maturity and patience. Keeping cool when reservations are lost, the bus breaks down, or during any of hundreds of potential travel crises is another prerequisite.

Although there are no specific educational requirements, most tour guides have a background in the travel industry, particularly front-line positions involving daily public contact. Others work in people-related fields like teaching or nursing. They may start small, by leading tours on a volunteer basis or working part-time. Pay begins at around $18,000 a year, topping out at $60,000, with the average being approximately $40,000 annually. Local hourly rates range from $8 to $12 an hour, with multilingual guides earning more.

Jobs are available with local sightseeing companies and attractions, travel agencies and cruise lines, and special interest, regional, and inbound tour organizations. Tour managers can also stay within their own geographical area and market their services to tourists through convention and visitors' bureaus and other outlets. You can be based anywhere, but you must truly be a citizen of the world, or at least of the place where you're giving tours.

Associations

American Society of Travel Agents
1101 King Street
Alexandria, VA 22314
703/739-2732

International Tour Management Institute
625 Market Street, Suite 1015
San Francisco, CA 94105
415/957-9489

International Guide Academy
Foote Hall, Suite 313
7150 Montview Blvd.
Denver, CO 80220
303/794-3048

Travel Industry Association of America
2 Lafayette Center
1133 21st Street, NW, Suite 800
Washington, DC 20036
202/408-8422

Books

Exploring Careers in the Travel Industry. Grant, Edgar. New York: Rosen, 1989.

Travel. Miller, Robert. Princeton, NJ: Peterson's, 1993.

The Vacation and Travel Tour Guidebook. Tripepi, Rocco. Greensboro, NC: Tudor, 1990.

Worldwide Tours. Davidoff, Philip and Doris. Englewood Cliffs, NJ: Prentice-Hall, 1990.

Your Career in Travel, Tourism, and Hospitality. Stevens, Laurence. Albany, NY: Delmar, 1988.

Magazines

Tour Operators and Promoters
Tour Trade
Travel Trade (magazine and newspaper editions)
Travel Market Report

Helga Pennington
Tour Guide

Experience as a flight attendant on international routes provided Helga Pennington of Kansas City, Missouri with the impetus to become a tour guide. "In a way," she says, "I'm more familiar with the world than my own neighborhood—I understand the paperwork, how to check into a hotel, and who to contact when you need to get things done. Each country is different." Easier to list would be the spots she *hasn't* been.

Pennington is also sensitive to the nationality of her clients, who are mostly from the United States. "Americans have their own cultural references and background and often feel intimidated being in an ancient society. So I need to figure out a way to make the group happy." This requires maturity: "Many of the best tour guides start out in their thirties."

> Nothing is really work unless you would rather be doing something else.
>
> —J. M. BARRIE

True Odds and Ends

Funeral Director
Handwriting Analyst/Graphologist
Mapmaker
Product Tester
Toll Collector

Funeral Director

This job is almost as tough to break into as acting. Most funeral directors inherit or marry into the business, with a few buying their way into existing operations after a long apprenticeship. Plus, each state has a different licensing procedure, so you're not exactly mobile. And you're on call day and night.

Still, the pay is decent: the average salary is in the $30,000 range, not including the profit from the funeral home if you're the owner. It's also very rewarding if you like to help people; you're providing a service in their hour of need. Most funeral directors are well-respected community members and get to wear nice clothes all the time. Those with an artistic flair may even enjoy restoration (many morticians are also embalmers), arranging the flowers sent to honor the deceased, and other matters of design. Since death takes no holidays, you're guaranteed a steady clientele.

Most states require that aspiring morticians be over twenty-one with a high school diploma or equivalent, graduate from a funeral service college, serve a one- to two-year apprenticeship, and pass the state board examination (college is a requirement in some states). You study anatomy, pathology, and physiology as well as embalming, restorative art, and mortuary administration and law. Such skills aren't easily transferred, so you should have a job lined up after your training and apprenticeship.

Those who want to start their own funeral homes should be prepared to invest several hundred thousand dollars, not only for the physical plant itself, but for specialized equipment like operating tables and draining facilities, embalming apparatus and supplies, and wheeled tables for moving the deceased. The home will need several well-furnished public rooms, such as a chapel for services, a display area for caskets and other funeral merchandise (clothing, urns), a viewing chamber for the body, and an office for meetings with families. This doesn't include the rental or purchase of limos used for transport.

Along with comforting families and embalming, a mortician makes arrangements with the cemetery for interment of the body and for the death certificate, contacts newspapers regarding details of the funeral, and makes sure the service and burial run smoothly. Those who do it well are guaranteed repeat customers, from among the living, that is.

Associations

Associated Funeral Directors Service International
P.O. Box 23023
St. Petersburg, FL 33742
813/579-1113

National Funeral Director Association
11121 W. Oklahoma Ave.
Milwaukee, WI 53227-4096
414/541-2500

National Foundation of Funeral Services
2250 E. Devon Ave., Suite 240
Des Plaines, IL 60018
708/827-6337

National Selected Morticians
1616 Central Street
Evanston, IL 60201
708/475-3414

Books

The Funeral Director's Financial Handbook. Plowe, Mort C. Englewood Cliffs, N.J.: Prentice-Hall, 1983.

The Funeral Director's Practice Management Handbook. Raether, Howard C., ed. Englewood Cliffs, N.J.: Prentice-Hall, 1989.

Sourcebook on Death and Dying. Chicago: Marquis Professional Publications, 1982 (includes state requirements).

Magazines

American Funeral Director
Cremationist of North America
Director
Embalmer
Funeral Service Insider

Al Carpenter
New Age Funeral Director

Along with running a funeral home, pastor-turned-mortician Al Carpenter of Alameda, California, sells inexpensive blueprints for do-it-yourself coffins. According to Carpenter they are "splendid grief therapy. Elderly people and families of those whose death is imminent find them especially meaningful."

Carpenter's funeral home is a no-frills operation: He meets with families in a simple office, sells urns made by a local potter, and charges only a few hundred dollars for a casket and slightly more for a full burial, while other mortuaries ask thousands for identical services. "I buy from the same place as the others, but I figure a marginal profit and don't have the overhead." Carpenter also discourages families from embalming their loved ones. "Not only do embalmers do terrible things to the body but the fluid is full of carcinogenic chemicals which go into the ground and can seep into the water supply.

"In the thirteen years I was in the ministry, I spoke at many funerals. It was a lot of pomp, circumstance, and needless expense. Now I'm helping people not only save money but deal realistically with death."

Handwriting Analyst/Graphologist

People can do wonders with facelifts, liposuction, and dye jobs, but they'd be hard-pressed to disguise their handwriting. In a sense, your signature is just like your fingerprint: It stays the same throughout the years unless you suffer neurological damage. And it reveals a lot about you—your abilities, attitudes, moods, and beliefs.

Those with an eye for detail and a fascination with human nature may find this an engrossing and rather lucrative occupation. You can provide services to attorneys, corporations, and agencies at between $100 to $400 per consultation, or charge up to $75 per hour. Individual handwriting appraisals range from $25 to $100 or even more, depending on geographical area.

Along with furnishing an objective character evaluation, graphologists help prospective employers screen for potential criminals and drug abuse. Handwriting analysis can assess leadership, social and cognitive abilities, and can assist in career counseling. Lawyers, and occasionally police, also use it to examine altered or forged documents, as well as threatening letters, false affidavits, and other questionable papers. Graphologists sometimes appear in court as expert witnesses and can influence the outcome of criminal and divorce cases.

This field is more of a science than an art and requires a course of study and certification. Classes can usually be taken at home and run about eighteen months. The student learns how to correlate slants, hooks, loops, swirls, and spaces with character traits. Because handwriting is done automatically, most forgeries are fairly easy to spot because the small muscles in the hand tense and quiver and it shows. Also, anytime a signature overlays another perfectly, it's a forgery. People never sign their name exactly the same way twice.

Sometimes, however, you may need to examine a document more closely and authenticate such things as paper, typewriting, or ink. Lab equipment—a microscope, magnifying glasses and lenses, halogen lights, a fluorescent light table, a protractor, and an engineering compass to determine size and spacing of letters along with photocopying and photo/video devices—can be essential. Equipment can run into the thousands of dollars, so it's best to start with a microscope and magnifiers and borrow or rent the rest as needed. Courses are also available on document verification, a separate discipline.

Because they are dealing with confidential information, graphologists must inspire trust in their clients and treat their chosen field like a business and not a novelty or fortune-telling scheme.

Associations

International Graphological Society
3685 Ingleside Drive
Dallas, TX 75229
214/351-3668

National Association of Document Examiners
47 Blauvelt Ave.
Dumont, NJ 07628
201/679-8257

National Bureau of Document Examiners
National Society for Graphology
250 W. 57th Street, Suite 2032
New York, NY 10107
212/265-1148

Books

The ABCs of Handwriting Analysis. Santoy, Claude. New York: Paragon House, 1989.
Graphology Explained. Branston, Barry. York Beach, ME: S. Weiser, 1991.
Handwriting and Personality. Mahony, Ann. New York: Holt, 1990.
The Psychological Basis of Handwriting Analysis. Lester, David. Chicago: Nelson Hall, 1981.
The Write Stuff. Beyerstein, Barry, ed. Buffalo NY: Prometheus, 1992.

Magazines

The Exemplar
The Write-Up

Don Lehew
Document Examiner

Dallas-based Don Lehew has been a contractor, an athletic director, and an owner of a private employment agency. Today, as a handwriting expert, he mostly makes his living dealing with forgers, angry spouses, drunks, murderers, and disgruntled employees—on paper, of course. He has given opinions in over two hundred cases in which documents have been questioned and has testified dozens of times in courts in Texas and California.

One particular dispute involved a letter containing sexual allegations. "It was my job to establish that an employee was making up accusations about her supervisor and in fact had written the letter even though she denied doing so." Lehew proved her to be the author, and the supervisor won a $17 million lawsuit for being slandered and unjustly fired.

He's not about to change jobs again (he hunts rattlesnakes, sky dives, and walks on the high wire for diversion). "When the phone rings, I never know who—or what—is going to be on the other end."

Mapmaker

Thanks to computers, airplanes, and satellites, mapmaking or cartography, has actually become easier. The Global Positioning System locates points on the earth via radio signals and transmits the information through satellites; the Global Information System provides computerized banks of spatial data; and improved aerial photography supplies enhanced and accurate images. Computers also trace boundaries and coastlines, provide printouts of map projections, and produce different statistical maps. Christopher Columbus never had it so good.

Still, along with an increased familiarity with computers, this job requires excellent spatial sense, precision, and an eye for detail. Most new maps, especially smaller ones, simply add information to an existing outline, or base map. New data from surveys or other sources are turned over to the mapmaker for incorporation and interpretation. Still, you may need to do additional research by going to the site and taking notes or looking up state and county land records.

Any attempt to transfer the round earth onto a flat surface can be fraught with errors that grow proportionally larger with the area covered. Put a town a fraction of a centimeter away from its exact point, and the users of the map will have trouble finding it.

Most cartographers have a B.A. in engineering, physical science, or geography with a special emphasis on mapping theory. Classes include the history of mapping, interpretation of maps, map design and projection, aerial mapping, surveying, and statistics. Vocational schools offer courses in map drafting and reproduction, as well as in basic photogrammetry, a related field dealing with the preparation of maps from the interpretation of aerial photographs using analysis and mathematical formulas.

Those wishing to become photogrammetrists take many of the same college courses as cartographers. They boldly go where no mapmaker has charted before, providing detailed maps of inaccessible or difficult to survey areas. They may find a greater demand for their services as satellites bring back pictures of distant planets.

The federal government is the biggest employer and the usual starting point for many cartographers, and the Department of Defense and the U.S. Geological Survey are the major source of jobs. Income begins at around $20,000 per annum, and doubles with years of experience. Those working for private firms, or in a specialty, can earn more from their charts. State and county agencies also hire cartographers.

Although this field has changed drastically over the past two thousand years, mapmakers still need artistic ability. Maps are used for just about everything—navigation, world events, the weather, even hiking trails—and people want to look at something aesthetically pleasing during their journeys.

Associations

American Congress of Surveying and Mapping
5410 Grosvenor Lane
Bethesda, MD 20814
301/493-0200

Books

Cartographic Methods. Lawrence, G. R. P. New York: Methuen, 1979.

Elements of Cartography. Robinson, Arthur H., et al. New York: Wiley, 1984.

Fundamentals of Cartography. Misra, R.P. New Delhi, India: Concept, 1989.

How Maps Are Made. Baynes, John. New York: Facts on File, 1987.

Mapping It Out. Monmonier, Mark. Chicago: University of Chicago, 1993.

Magellen Mapping Module. Miller, Cynthia A. Pasadena, CA: National Aeronautics and Space Administration, nd.

Magazines

Cartographica
Cartography and Geographic Information Systems

G-Map
GIS Mapline
Mapping Sciences and Remote Survey

John Snyder
Cartographer

John Snyder of Sandy Springs, Maryland, got into his field by dabbling. "I was trained as a chemical engineer and worked for three different companies," he says. "But I was always interested in mapmaking." In 1976, he attended a lecture about the difficulty of obtaining mathematical map projections from satellite imagery, and as a volunteer, came up with a solution. He was hired by the U.S. Geological Survey (USGS) a few years later.

For a while, Snyder juggled two careers, but today he works part-time for the USGS and is the author of several books on cartography and history. As someone who is basically self-taught, Snyder regards himself as the exception rather than the rule. "Most cartographers aren't interested in the mathematical aspects, so I was glad to put together the information." But still, "They need to be well-rounded in the technical side," he explains, "and keep themselves constantly up-to-date."

Product Tester

Products don't just materialize on store shelves. Someone has to go out and actually test powders, creams, soaps, toothpastes, deodorants, over-the-counter medications such as antacids and aspirin, and even feminine hygiene spray. You can earn some bucks, \$5 to \$150, depending upon the study and amount of time and effort involved, and receive free samples of the product (unless you got the placebo). Plus, you have a say in what works and what doesn't.

After all, manufacturers such as Proctor and Gamble, Colgate-Palmolive, and Lever Brothers have to back up their claims. If they say their foot spray lasts longer than a competitor's, it must be proven with a scientific study. Sometimes they find, much to their dismay, that the opposite is true. Lucky for them research and development labs are big on confidentiality.

Although it pays to be a human guinea pig, don't expect to make a living at it, unless you're one of a handful of individuals who works full-time in a lab, sniffing armpits and other body parts. Before you get too excited, the lab explicitly states they want absolutely no publicity.

At one time or another, most people can qualify for product studies if they live near a research laboratory that specializes in product testing. Many are located in the New York-New Jersey area, although there are a few in the Midwest and West as well. Other sources for subject testing—although it may be for scientific or psychological research—are large universities, such as Ohio State University in Columbus. Although University projects may not always pay cash, they often provide free room and board or other forms of compensation. Periodically, facilities run advertisements in the newspapers, looking for, say, women with arthritis for a pain reliever, men with gray hair for a new type of dye, or couples who are about to get married to measure their levels of stress.

Once labs know you're reliable, accurate, and provide honest and detailed information and evaluations, they file your name for future reference and call when an appropriate study arises. Normally, participation in studies is limited to once every thirty days, so products don't intermingle and affect each other's results. You may also be checked for blood pressure, pulse rate, etc. before participating. And you don't even have to pay the doctor.

Everything, including the possible side effects and potential dangers, is put in writing. But not to worry. By the time the product reaches you, the average American consumer, it likely has already been put through its paces with animals and in foreign countries.

Associations

International Testing and Evaluation Association
4400 Fair Lakes Court
Fairfax, VA 22033-3899
703/631-6220

Consumer Federation of America
1424 16th Street, NW, Suite 604
Washington, DC 20036
202/387-6121

Consumer Information Center
18 F Street, NW, Room G-142
Washington, DC 20405
202/501-1794

Also check the Yellow Pages under, "Laboratories, Research and Development."

Books

Advertising, Packaging, and Labeling. National Association of Consumer Agency Ads. Washington: U.S. Department of Commerce, nd.

Consumer Information Processing Research. Winkle, William L. Cambridge, MA: Marketing Science Institute, 1975.

Cosmetic and Toiletry Formulations. Flick, Ernest W. Park Ridge, NJ: Noyes, 1992.

Perfumes, Cosmetics, and Toiletries. Land, Eric. Washington, DC: U.S. International Trade Commission, 1993.

Magazines

Category Report
Product Alert
Product Safety Letter

Betty Carlson
Product Tester

Betty Carlson of Whitestone, New York, traces her "career" as a product tester back to the birth of her son, Christopher. "I was looking for a way to earn extra income without leaving the house or babysitting for other people's kids," she says. "This was the perfect solution."

Carlson takes her duties seriously. "If I'm testing a pain remedy, I wait until I get a headache, ingest the product, then set the timer for every fifteen minutes to see how I feel. I then grade it from one to ten on a scale of effectiveness." She has also tried new brands of perfume, toothpaste, and baby powder for Christopher.

"You need to be precise, know how to gauge a product, and have good writing skills," she continues. After all, Mr. and Ms. John Q. Public depend on her good judgment.

Toll Collector

This may *seem* like a boring job, but consider the following: Someone can run into and demolish your toll booth (and possibly you) with their vehicle; you may have to deal with wild animals or a pit bull that escaped from a car; or you may encounter the more dangerous, drunken two-legged version on the lam from the law. When they're not smiling, giving directions, and making change, toll collectors may be facing these very real scenarios.

And despite the fact that for eight or so hours you're crammed into a space the approximate size of a telephone booth, you may not be allowed to sit down during your shift, and you're exposed to the elements and whims of a public that's not keen on paying money to drive down the road, competition for these jobs is intense. (Position openings can be found in newspaper ads or through state employment listings.) For one thing, the work is steady. Although computers have replaced some of the more routine activities, there will always be a need for humans to make sure the toll system is extracting its fair share. Plus, pay starts at about $10 to $12 an hour, going up to about $15—and that's before overtime, longevity increases, and other incentives. A veteran collector can earn $35,000 or more a year. In addition, a turnpike is rather impervious to takeovers, recessions, and corporate transfers.

Still, the job is not all punching tickets and reading *People* magazine when things get slow. Toll collectors must be able to balance their cash box at the end of the day, operate the computer terminal to record all transactions, and provide accurate directions to just about anywhere in the state. This includes knowledge of road construction, rush-hour traffic patterns and suggestions for alternate routes. They must also be able to classify vehicles based on axle size and weight so they can determine how much to charge. According to experienced toll collectors, errors and rude retorts usually have a way of coming back to haunt them; travelers don't hesitate to complain.

The job requires a high school education or equivalent. Qualifying usually involves passing a test of math and comprehension skills. Although training may take only a few days, you must be familiar with the rules and regulations of the road. These are often found in thick manuals and may take several months to learn. You must also be able to operate radio equipment.

Scenarios involving drunk drivers, hitchhikers, stolen or unsafe vehicles, and other potential dangers are reported to local law enforcement officials, and are not handled by the collector. Although you may be wearing a uniform, working odd hours, and dealing with strange characters, all similarities to the police end there.

Associations

International Bridge, Tunnel and Turnpike
Association
2120 L Street, NW, Suite 305
Washington, DC 20037
202/659-4620

Books

Congressional Intent and Road User Payments. Bhatt, Kiran. Washington: Urban Institute, 1977.
Transportation Improvement and Road Pricing. Bhatt, Kiran, et al. Washington: Urban Institute, 1976.

Magazines

International Bridge
Tunnel and Turnpike Proceedings
Public Roads
Tollways

Gary Cawley
Toll Collections Superintendent

Before he started as a toll collector in 1979, Gary Cawley of the Ohio Turnpike Commission in Berea, Ohio, held over a dozen different jobs. "I worked in factories and in the auto industry," he recalls. "But toll collecting is unique. You meet someone once and give them directions. You may never see them again, but they'll associate you with the area." Although Ohio Turnpike employees are not hired by the state, "people perceive us as representatives of Ohio, so we place a great deal of emphasis on courtesy and helpfulness."

The job can be tedious at times and seem confining, but "it's what you make it. You're meeting and working with all kinds of people. You may be alone in the toll booth, but you're never far from your coworkers or a help station."

> Writing is easy; all you do is sit staring at a blank sheet of paper until the drops of blood form on your forehead.
>
> —GENE FOWLER

Wordsmiths (and Joneses)

Article Clipper
Greeting Card Writer
Indexer
Novelist

Article Clipper

Anybody can read, right? (Well, at least anyone who's reading this book.) Corporations; high-profile individuals, such as celebrities and the wealthy; trade, technical, and professional journals; and consumer publications all want to know what's being published about them or their field and may utilize a clipping service. What seems like the easiest job in the world—perusing newspaper and magazine articles and sending them to these clients—can actually be quite intricate and frustrating.

Depending upon your duties, you may be culling data on thousands of subjects from hundreds of written sources or references for a few, hard-to-find items. Plus, you can't really get involved with what you're reading or you might miss an essential reference. This job takes a special kind of person who can sit quietly for hours on end and even makes a solitary activity like writing look like the NCAA Final Four.

Although an article clipping service is inexpensive to start up (desk, card file, typing paper, envelopes), you have serious competition from the major players like Bacon's and Burrelle's as well as from computer information services like CompuServe and America Online that provide an immense amount of written data on just about every subject. Like McDonald's, information is cheap and ubiquitous. Those who take time to study publications and their specific needs, however, can make from $1 to $50 per clipping sold. You will need access to primary material—neighborhood newspapers, obscure and small journals—not found in major sources.

Those wishing to pursue this job, or who hope to start their own business, can receive the best training from an existing clipping service. Over a period of several weeks, you are taught scanning techniques—that is, looking for buzz words instead of reading for content—how to judge what's relevant, and other tricks of the trade. According to one long-term clipping service employee, many are called but few survive the initial six months. After that, turnover is minimal.

Article clippers must also be self-motivated (only you know what you've *really* looked at) and flexible. Sometimes a headline or the first few paragraphs may not seem appropriate, but a quick skim throughout will reveal important references. Memory may work against you in this job, because you may dismiss an article too easily.

Still, clippers are paid well—$15,000 to $30,000 per year with the larger services. And just about any educational background is acceptable, even a GED. So if you enjoy solitude and can't remember a darn thing at the end of the day, you may be "cut out" for this career.

Associations

International Federation of Press Cutting Agencies
Steulistrasse 19
CH-8030
Zurich, Switzerland

Books

Automating the Newspaper Clipping Files. Newspaper Division, Special Libraries Association. Washington, DC: The Association, 1987.

Starting and Operating a Clipping Service. Smith, Demaris. Babylon, NY: Pilot, 1987.

Also directories, such as *Bacon's International Media Directory, Burrelle's Consumer Trade Publication Directory, Gale Directory of Publications and Broadcast Media*, and others

Magazines

Followup File
The Cole Papers
Information Broker
Working Press of the Nation

Kaye Gambral
Clipping Supervisor

Computers play a big part at Bacon's Information Incorporated in Rockford, Illinois. "When article clippers see a buzz word for a particular trade, a proper name, or an association, they type it into the system," says Kaye Gambral. The screen then calls up the specifics—what papers the clients want information from, for example—and any restrictions. If the article fits the requirements, the clipper then marks it to be sent.

"Clippers must be detail-oriented, observant, and aware," she goes on. "They're mentally on their toes eight hours a day." But Gambral knows she has a problem when she overhears someone talking about what they read in the break room. "If they retain information, they got too involved and lost their scanning concentration." Still, "no one is 100 percent accurate all the time."

Clippers must meet a certain quota, which depends heavily on the content of the publication. Obviously those that are more complex or contain a greater number of names and references take longer to pore over.

Even though she's a supervisor, Gambral pitches in when things get busy. "I'm responsible for making sure people do their work correctly and complete the job on time."

Greeting Card Writer

Greeting card writers must send their very best . . . for companies to accept their submissions. These may exclude the big three—Hallmark, Gibson, and American Greetings—who sometimes refuse all unsolicited manuscripts. But plenty of smaller regional and specialty "niche" companies are looking for deathless rhymed and unrhymed verse. And with an average pay of $50 to $100 per acceptance (up to $250 from a major corporation), sales of your nuggets of inspiration can gather some green stuff.

But as with most forms of writing, this is more difficult than it looks and is quite different from dashing off a poem about a long-lost love or misbegotten youth. You must first consider the category—whether it's *traditional* (Christmas, Thanksgiving, Mother's Day, etc.), expressing conventional, generalized feelings or *studio or contemporary*, covering the same basic areas but with an unorthodox twist. These cards may also deal with current topics. Or, the category can be *alternative*, voicing sentiment about anything from a promotion to a divorce to the death of a pet. These can also be humorous or risqué.

Then you need to identify theme and style. Is it about love or friendship? Should the lines be iambic pentameter or free verse? Another factor to consider is relationship—whether it's from a daughter to a mother, a generic card for an acquaintance, a greeting "from the gang," and so on.

A great assisting in this process is a book called *Writer's Market* (see below), which lists the various card companies and their overall requirements. Contact each business for detailed guidelines, catalog, and a market list before mailing in submissions, always enclosing a self-addressed stamped envelope (SASE). There's no faster turnoff than sending a dozen flowery prose pieces for Valentine's Day to a group specializing in satire. You may also be asked to sign a disclosure agreement, stating your ideas are original and have not been submitted elsewhere.

Most material is presented on index cards, each with your name and address, card category/theme/relationship, the verse itself, and a code for your personal records. (Card writers may be circulating dozens of ideas at a time, so a log helps keep things straight). Submissions can be made in batches of five to twenty, with the strongest verses on top. And, again, enclose an SASE, or you may never see your stuff again. Suggestions for accompanying art are usually welcome; requirements vary for actual photos and illustrations.

If the company buys an idea, they will likely take all rights. This may involve licensing for gift items, so the concept can appear on everything from mugs to T-shirts. As the author, you might be able to negotiate a small royalty.

The essence of a great card is that it appeals to a wide audience yet seems written exclusively for the individual reader. The best place to get a feel for the market is *at* the market—a grocery store, card shop, anywhere cards are sold. Retailers will tell you what's popular. Then, it's how you play your cards.

Associations

Greeting Card Association
1200 G Street, NW, Suite 760
Washington, DC 20005
202/393-1778

Books

The Complete Guide to Greeting Card Design and Illustration. Szela, Eva. Cincinnati: North Light, 1987.
Freelance Writing for Greeting Card Companies. Stauss, Patrisha. Plantation, FL: Distinctive, 1993.
The Greeting Card Handbook. Hohman, Edward, and Norma Leary. New York: Barnes and Noble, 1981.
How to Write and Sell Greeting Cards, Bumper Stickers, T-Shirts, and Other Fun Stuff. Wigand, Molly. Cincinnati: Writer's Digest, 1992.
Writer's Market. Cincinnati: Writer's Digest, updated annually.

Magazines

Greetings
Greetings Magazine Buyers Guide
Party and Paper Retailer

Suzanne Heins
Greeting Card Staff Writer

Like thousands of others before her (and since) Suzanne Heins of Hallmark Cards in Kansas City, Missouri, submitted a portfolio of writing samples hoping she would be hired as a greeting card writer. "I came at a time when they decided to expand their staff," says the eight-year veteran, modestly.

Heins was an English major, but her coworkers come from diverse backgrounds. "Education doesn't seem to matter. You either have the knack or you don't."

Still, "I had to learn to accept rejection. A lot of what's written has been done before. You need to continually come up with a fresh approach."

Heins likes the fact that her job accentuates the positive. "You're not out there telling someone they have bad breath, that they need this mouthwash. Your words are helping them express their innermost feelings."

Indexer

This job requires knowledge from A to Z and all points between. Along with subject matter expertise and a strong educational background, indexers need patience, attention to detail, and a passion for order. They must work quickly and accurately against tight deadlines, since the index is the last thing completed before a book goes to press. Mistakes are permanent—at least for the life of the printing—and out there for the whole world to see. The bonus is that you can set your own hours and work at home.

Although there are two basic types of indexes—list and paragraph style—each has varying levels of complexity and dozens of permutations. Also, publishers have their own specific requirements. So indexers either need to be extremely well-versed in the subject at hand or in the mechanics of indexing, preferably both. This is one job where you can't just look busy.

Some indexers are self-taught, although many have taken classes through library school, the U.S. Department of Agriculture (USDA), and at colleges and universities. At under three hundred dollars apiece, the USDA courses on basic and applied indexing are a bargain. Classes in information storage and retrieval, research methods, and in classification and cataloging are also helpful.

Pay can be by the entry, the page, or the hour. Subject matter, depth of information, and use of terminology are all considered when setting fees. For instance, indexing a collection of essays on dog ownership is very different from indexing a textbook on artificial intelligence. On the average, however, indexers earn between $20 and $50 an hour.

You can still do an index by annotating, organizing, and alphabetizing each entry on a three by five card, but computers have greatly simplified the task of marking, editing, and cross-referencing entries. Sophisticated software packages double-check your work and spelling, in addition to sorting and formatting additions. But you will still need to read through each page, possibly several times, marking relevant words and phrases and noting themes. You then decide where you saw a subject before, how it will fit in with the overall index, and whether it should be combined under a larger heading.

Between purchasing computer equipment and getting the proper training, launching yourself as an indexer may cost a couple of thousand dollars. But the payoff comes when publishers, periodicals, and even corporations, who occasionally need an index for their written products, start calling. You have the final word, and like the index itself, the money can add up quickly.

Associations

American Society of Indexers
Membership Department
P.O. Box 386
Port Aransas, TX 78323
512/749-4052

American Council on Education
Library and Information Services
1 Dupont Circle NW
Washington, DC 20036
202/939-9405

U.S. Department of Agriculture
Correspondence Program
Graduate School, USDA
AG Box 9911
Washington, DC 20250-9911
202/720-7123

Books

The Chicago Manual of Style. 14th ed. Chicago: University of Chicago, 1993.

Handbook of Indexing Techniques: A Guide for Beginning Indexers. Fetters, Linda. Port, Aransas, TX: author, 1994.

Indexing Books. Mulvaney, Nancy. Chicago: University of Chicago, 1994.

Indexing Concepts and Methods. Borko, Harold and Charles Bernier. New York: Academic, 1978.

Indexing From A to Z. Wellisch, Hans. Bronx, New York: Wilson, 1991.

Introduction to Indexing and Abstracting. Cleveland, Donale and Ana. Englewood, CO: Libraries Unlimited, 1990.

Magazines

Indexer
Information America
Key Words: The Newsletter of ASI

Linda Fetters
Indexer

Indexing is the ideal job for Linda Fetters of Port Aransas, Texas. "Each index is different," says the seventeen-year veteran. "Whenever I talk to another indexer or work for a different publisher, I learn something new."

Still, the job is not without stress. "You must learn how to deal with deadlines and juggle several different projects. You may find yourself working seven days a week and as many hours as needed to get the assignment done."

Indexers can come from any walk of life. "Most are widely read, with a lot of curiosity. They must comprehend what they are indexing so they can condense information into a concise, usable form."

Novelist

There are two parts to becoming a novelist: writing the book and selling it. Both can be equally difficult and frustrating. But at least getting started is cheap: All you need is imagination, paper, and an old typewriter (even the most computer phobic usually end up with a word processor, however).

Although the term *best-selling novelist* evokes talk shows, readings where the audience hangs on your deathless prose, and autograph sessions at bookstores, the cold reality is that you must apply your seat to a chair and write. Then you send your brainchild to several publishers. You check the mailbox every afternoon, expecting a large advance, and indeed one day something does arrive—your manuscript, with a rejection form letter.

At this point, many people give up. Or they go back to writing the same thing over and over again, never showing it to anyone. Or they simply think about writing, and attend writers' conferences and literary functions. But you can't really learn anything or improve unless you give your book to someone who *does* know how to write (not a friend, relative, or neighbor) and listen to his comments. And read all the fiction you can, from classics to contemporary novels.

It's like school all over again. Some of it you will discard, but the basic tools of fiction—character, dialogue, plot, and setting—will become understandable and logical. During this process of discovery, you may find a type of fiction writing you do especially well. There are several genres: science fiction, horror, romance, westerns, mystery, suspense, and the legal blockbuster, recently pioneered by Scott Turow and John Grisham. And genres are a lot easier to sell than Great American Novels.

The best places to get help are universities, which feature evening, weekend, and part-time programs, and reputable writers' conferences, where established authors work with novices, sometimes for several weeks. Correspondence schools are another option. The most well-known is the Writers' Digest School, but be wary of wild claims made by some of the others. Paid critics are an even less dependable route; you'll be writing the book to please them, not editors or readers. Always check references and previous clients.

Once you've got your novel where you want it (usually after several rewrites and edits), you can send it to a publisher who handles the same type of book. *Writer's Market* and *Literary Market Place (LMP)* list hundreds of publishers, along with providing names, addresses, and preferences; the magazine *Publisher's Weekly* tells who's buying what. Should your book be accepted, be prepared for not only revisions but for the fact that you, the author, have little or no input on the title, cover, or way it's promoted (if at all).

Another way to publication is through a literary agent. This presents the old chicken-and-egg question: It's tough to find a publisher without an agent and most agents are extremely selective in choosing unpublished writers. The library has listings of agents who handle authors with sensibilities similar to yours.

And who knows? Your name (or pseudonym) may end up in every bookstore and library in America.

Associations

American Society of Journalists and Authors
1501 Broadway, Suite 302
New York, NY 10036
212/997-0947

Author's Guild
234 West 44th Street
New York, NY 10036
212/398-0838

National Writer's Union
Suite 203
8073 Broadway
New York, NY 10003
212/254-0279

Books

The Apprentice Writer. Green, Julian. New York: M. Boyars, 1993.

Characters and Viewpoint. Card, Orson Scott, Cincinnati: Writer's Digest, 1988.

How To Write a Damn Good Novel. Frey, James and Mark Washburn. New York: St. Martins, 1994.

Literary Market Place. New York: Bowker, updated annually.

Plot. Dibell, Ansen. Cincinnati: Writer's Digest, 1988.

Scene and Structure. Bickham, Jack. Cincinnati: Writer's Digest, 1993.

Turning Life Into Fiction. Hemley, Robin. Cincinnati: Story, 1994

The Weekend Novelist. Ray, Robert J. New York: Dell, 1994.

Writer's Market. Cincinnati: Writer's Digest, updated annually.

Magazines

Poet and Writer
Publisher's Weekly
The Writer
Writer's Digest

Judith Kelman
Suspense Writer

Judith Kelman is an inspiration to anyone who's never taken a writing course: the bestselling suspense novelist's paperbacks command six-figure advances and she's entirely self-taught. A former speech therapist, Kelman quit her day job eleven years ago and began writing newspaper and magazine articles and novels, "anything I could think of," she says. "Had I needed to, I would have written fortune cookies."

After giving her first book a "well-deserved burial," Kelman started on and finished her second, selling it through an agent in two weeks. Subsequent titles include *The House on the Hill, Someone's Watching, Hush Little Darlings, While Angels Sleep, If I Should Die*, and others.

Although prolific, the New Jersey-based author revises and cuts the length of her books several times before submitting them to her editor. Of the writing process she says, "It's like juggling six machetes at once. Not only do the various elements of fiction need to be balanced, but any novel can have a number of outcomes and I have to choose the right one." Kelman writes a lot more than appears in her final draft: "I need to get a feel for my characters and know as much about them as possible." Her books are extensively researched.

Even though a novel may never see publication, "nothing is lost," she points out. "You've made a significant effort toward mastering the craft. No one expects you to make a perfect sweater on the first try, so why should a first or even second book be any different?"

Appendix

Some (Very) Brief Checklists for Working on Your Own

Millions of trees have been sacrificed regarding the subjects of part-time and alternative work and being your own boss. So rather than add to the depletion of our forests, the following lists are just some starting points when considering nontraditional jobs. A bibliography and additional reading resources are included at the end of this chapter.

Motivational needs

- Self-starter
- Good organizational skills
- Willingness to spend time on the job
- Ability to keep good records
- Discipline, ability to meet deadlines
- Fondness for people, animals, or whatever you're working with
- Ability to follow through
- Ability to stick with a path, even if the initial payoff isn't great
- Belief in self, product, or service
- Willingness to take chances

Financial and other challenges

- Evening, weekend hours
- Phone calls, interruptions at odd times
- Purchase of own equipment or franchise
- Overhead costs, such as rental of space, phone, electricity

- May have to hire, handle, and keep records on employees
- Ability to deal with rejection or skepticism
- May have to take an additional job to supplement income during start-up

Financial and legal questions

- What kind of insurance will be needed?
- What kind of permits and licenses are required by the state, city, or county?
- Is there a need or market for the product or service?
- How do I set the price?
- Is there adequate capital, or savings, if things get tight?
- How will I handle tax records? Should I hire an accountant? What about deductibles?
- What kind of legal issues are involved? Is a lawyer needed? If applicable:
    - What about materials and supplies?
    - What about publicity and advertising?
    - If I decide to set up shop at home, what about zoning laws?

Some suggestions

- If at home:
    - Set up your own work space, including an answering machine with adult voice mail, not a child's.
    - Arrange for child care; attempting to do the job right and meeting youngsters' constant needs don't mix.
- Establish certain hours to be "on the job."
- Get everything in writing, particularly money matters.
- Have a business plan and evaluate periodically how well you're doing.
- Maintain and keep in touch with a network of contacts.
- Learn as much as possible about, and keep up with, the field, going to conventions, seminars, and interest group meetings.
- Find out about the local economy, particularly your immediate competition.

- Make sure this what you *really* love. Only a select few find fame and fortune in their true vocation!

Bibliography

Drake, Barbara. *Starting a Business in Your Own Home* (handout). Columbus, OH: Cooperative Extension Service, Ohio State University, nd.

Fox, Paul G. *Thriving in Tough Times.* Hawthorne, NJ: Career Press, 1992.

Gumpert, David E. "Doing a Little Business on the Side." *Working Woman* (October 1985) 41-45.

Wise, Nicole. "Successful Strategies for Part-Time Work." *Parents* (December 1988) 70-79.

Suggested Reading

Changing Careers. Sikula, Lola. Pacific Grove, CA: Brooks/Cole, 1993.

College Majors and Careers. Phifer, Paul. Garrett Park, MD: Garrett Park, 1993.

The Encyclopedia of Career Choices for the Nineties. New York: Perigee, 1992.

The Encyclopedia of Careers and Vocational Guidance. Hopke, William, ed. Chicago: J. G. Ferguson, 1993.

The Part-Time Job Book. Pell, Arthur. New York: Monarch, 1984.

Where the Jobs Are. Wright, John W., with Don Clippinger. New York: Avon, 1992.

The Work-at-Home Sourcebook. Arden, Lynne. Boulder: Live Oak, 1994.

VGM's Careers Checklists. Hirsch, Arlene S. Lincolnwood, IL: National Textbook, 1991.

Want a New, Better, Fantastic Job? Gross, Pam and Peter Paskill. Lake Oswego, OR: RightSide Resources, 1991.

Working From the Heart. McMakin, Jacqueline with Sonya Dyer. San Francisco: HarperCollins, 1993.